Important Instruction

D1200040

Students, Parents, and Teachers can use the URL or ......code provided below to access two full-length Lumos MAAP practice tests. Please note that these assessments are provided in the Online format only.

URL	QR Code
Visit the URL below and place the book access code **http://www.lumoslearning.com/a/tedbooks** **Access Code: G4MMAAP-25197-S**	

lumos learning
Developed by Expert Teachers

Mississippi Academic Assessment Program (MAAP) Online Assessments and 4th Grade Math Practice Workbook, Student Copy

Contributing Author	-	**Jessica Fisher**
Contributing Author	-	**Wilma Muhammad**
Executive Producer	-	**Mukunda Krishnaswamy**
Designer and Illustrator	-	**Harini N.**

COPYRIGHT ©2018 by Lumos Information Services, **LLC. ALL RIGHTS RESERVED.** No portion of this book may be reproduced mechanically, electronically or by any other means, including photocopying, recording, taping, Web Distribution or Information Storage and Retrieval systems, without prior written permission of the Publisher, Lumos Information Services, LLC.

First Edition - 2020

NGA Center/CCSSO are the sole owners and developers of the Common Core State Standards, which does not sponsor or endorse this product. © Copyright 2010. National Governors Association Center for Best Practices and Council of Chief State School Officers.

Mississippi Department of Education is not affiliated to Lumos Learning. Mississippi Department of Education, was not involved in the production of, and does not endorse these products or this site.

ISBN-10: 172279352X

ISBN-13: 978-1722793524

Printed in the United States of America

For permissions and additional information contact us

Lumos Information Services, LLC
PO Box 1575, Piscataway, NJ 08855-1575
http://www.LumosLearning.com

Email: support@lumoslearning.com
Tel: (732) 384-0146
Fax: (866) 283-6471

Developed by Expert Teachers

INTRODUCTION

This book is specifically designed to improve student achievement on the Mississippi Academic Assessment Program (MAAP) Test. With over a decade of expertise in developing practice resources for standardized tests, Lumos Learning has designed the most efficient methodology to help students succeed on the state assessments (See Figure 1).

Lumos Smart Test Prep Methodology provides students MAAP assessment rehearsal along with an efficient pathway to overcome any standards proficiency gaps. Students perform at their best on standardized tests when they feel comfortable with the test content as well as the test format. Lumos online practice tests are meticulously designed to mirror the MAAP assessment. It adheres to the guidelines provided by the MAAP for the number of questions, standards, difficulty level, sessions, question types, and duration.

The process starts with students taking the online diagnostic assessment. This online diagnostic test will help assess students' proficiency levels in various standards.

After completion of the diagnostic assessment, students can take note of standards where they are not proficient. This step will help parents and educators in developing a targeted remedial study plan based on a student's proficiency gaps.

Once the targeted remedial study plan is in place, students can start practicing the lessons in this workbook that are focused on specific standards.

After the student completes the targeted remedial practice, the student should attempt the second online MAAP practice test. Record the proficiency levels in the second practice test to measure the student progress and identify any additional learning gaps. Further targeted practice can be planned to help students gain comprehensive skills mastery needed to ensure success on the state assessment.

Lumos Smart Test Prep Methodology

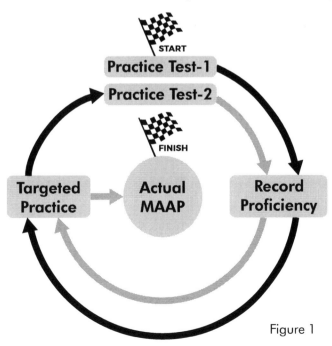

Figure 1

Table of Contents

Sign Up Online

MAAP

Grade 4 Math Practice

Unlock Digital Access

2 MAAP Practice Tests

5 Math Domains

Sign Up Now

Url: https://LumosLearning/a/tedbooks

Access Code: G4MMAAP-25197-S

Access MAAP Test Practice Resources On Your Mobile Device

Online Access

for

MAAP Practice

+

Printed Workbook

for

Skills Practice

Download Lumos StepUp App
from Google Play Store or Apple App Store

After installing the StepUp App, scan this **QR Code** via **tedBook** section of the mobile app

Chapter 1
Lumos Smart Test Prep Methodology

Step 1: Access Online MAAP Practice Test

The online MAAP practice tests mirror the actual Mississippi Academic Assessment Program in the number of questions, item types, test duration, test tools, and more.

After completing the test, your student will receive immediate feedback with detailed reports on standards mastery and a personalized study plan to overcome any learning gaps. With this study plan, use the next section of the workbook to practice.

Use the URL and access code provided below or scan the QR code to access the first MAAP practice test to get started.

URL	QR Code
Visit the URL below and place the book access code **http://www.lumoslearning.com/a/tedbooks** **Access Code: G4MMAAP-25197-S**	

Step-2: Review the Personalized Study Plan Online

After students complete the online Practice Test 1, they can access their individualized study plan from the table of contents (Figure 2) Parents and Teachers can also review the study plan through their Lumos account (parent or teacher) portal.

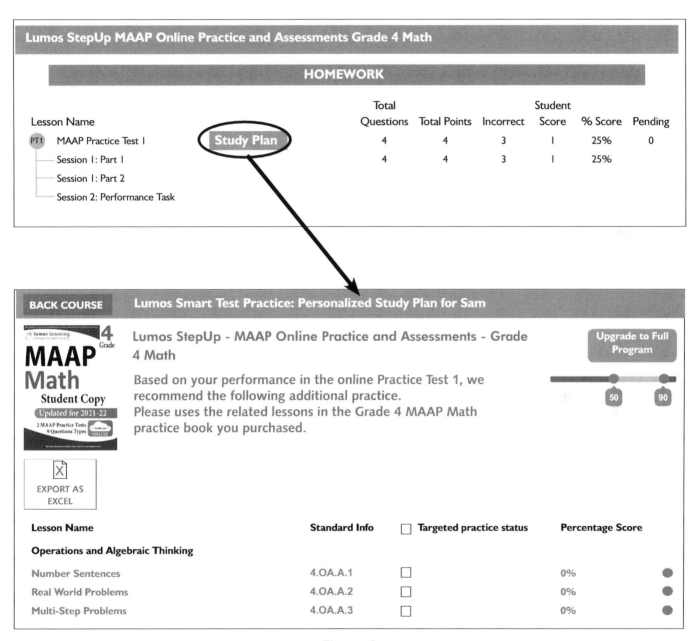

Figure 2

Step 3: Complete Targeted Practice

Using the information provided in the study plan report, complete the targeted practice using the appropriate lessons to overcome proficiency gaps. With lesson names included in the study plan, find the appropriate topics in this workbook and answer the questions provided. Marking the completed lessons in the study plan after each practice session is recommended.(See Figure 3)

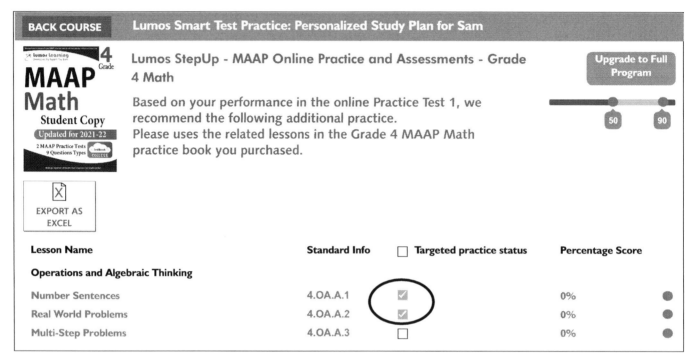

Figure 3

Step 4: Access the Practice Test 2 Online

After completing the targeted practice in this workbook, students should attempt the second MAAP practice test online. Using the student login name and password, login to the Lumos website to complete the second practice test.

Step 5: Repeat Targeted Practice

Repeat the targeted practice as per Step 3 using the second study plan report for Practice test 2 after completion of the second MAAP rehearsal.

Visit http://www.lumoslearning.com/a/lstp for more information on Lumos Smart Test Prep Methodology or Scan the QR Code

1) **The day before the test,** make sure you get a good night's sleep.

2) **On the day of the test,** be sure to eat a good hearty breakfast! Also, be sure to arrive at school on time.

3) **During the test:**

- **Read every question carefully.**

  - Do not spend too much time on any one question. Work steadily through all questions in the section.
  - Attempt all of the questions even if you are not sure of some answers.
  - If you run into a difficult question, eliminate as many choices as you can and then pick the best one from the remaining choices. Intelligent guessing will help you increase your score.
  - Also, mark the question so that if you have extra time, you can return to it after you reach the end of the section.
  - Some questions may refer to a graph, chart, or other kind of picture. Carefully review the infographics before answering the question.
  - Be sure to include explanations for your written responses and show all work.

- **While Answering EBSR questions.**

  - EBSR questions come in 2 parts - PART A and B.
  - Both PART A and B could be multiple choice or Part A could be multiple choice while Part B could be some other type.
  - Generally, Part A and B will be related, sometimes it may just be from the same lesson but not related questions.
  - If it is a Multiple choice question, Select the bubble corresponding to your answer choice.
  - Read all of the answer choices, even if think you have found the correct answer.
  - In case the questions in EBSR are not multiple choice questions, follow the instruction for other question types while answering such questions.

- **While Answering TECR questions.**

  - Read the directions of each question. Some might ask you to drag something, others to select, and still others to highlight. Follow all instructions of the question (or questions if it is in multiple parts)

Chapter 2:
Operations and Algebraic Thinking

Lesson 1: Number Sentences

You can scan the QR code given below or use the url to access additional EdSearch resources including videos and mobile apps related to *Number Sentences*.

Categories	About 9 results (0.034 seconds)

Videos (4)

Questions (3)

Khan Academy (2)

Popular Searches ▼

Recent Searches ▼

Comparing with multiplication

Resource: Khan Academy
Standard: 4.OA.A.1
Grade: 4
Subject: Math

Topic   Standard

+

---

ed Search   Number Sentences

URL	QR Code
http://www.lumoslearning.com/a/4oaa1	

1. Andrew is twice as old as his brother, Josh. Which equation could be used to figure out Andrew's age if Josh's age, n, is unknown?

   Ⓐ $a = n + 2$
   Ⓑ $a = n \div 2$
   Ⓒ $n = a + 2$
   Ⓓ $a = 2 \times n$

2. Mandy bought 28 marbles. She wants to give the same number of marbles to each of her four friends. What equation or number sentence would she use to find the number of marbles each friend will get?

   Ⓐ $28 - 4 = n$
   Ⓑ $28 \div 4 = n$
   Ⓒ $28 + 4 = n$
   Ⓓ $28 - 4 = n$

3. What number does n represent?
   $3 + 6 + n = 22$

   Ⓐ $n = 9$
   Ⓑ $n = 13$
   Ⓒ $n = 18$
   Ⓓ $n = 31$

4. Cindy's mother baked cookies for the school bake sale. Monday she baked 4 dozen cookies. Tuesday she baked 3 dozen cookies. Wednesday she baked 4 dozen cookies. After she finished baking Thursday afternoon, she took 15 dozen cookies to the bake sale. Which equation shows how to determine the number of cookies that she baked on Thursday?

   Ⓐ $4 + 3 + 4 + n = 15$
   Ⓑ $4 + 3 + 4 = n$
   Ⓒ $4 \times 3 \times 4 \times n = 15$
   Ⓓ $15 \div 11 = n$

5. There are 9 students in Mrs. Whitten's class. She gave each student the same number of popsicle sticks. There were 47 popsicle sticks in her bag. To decide how many sticks each student received, Larry wrote the following number sentence: $47 \div 9 = n$. How many popsicle sticks were left in the bag after dividing them evenly among the 9 students?

   Ⓐ 0
   Ⓑ 2
   Ⓒ 3
   Ⓓ 4

6. Sixty-three students visited the science exhibit. The remainder of the visitors were adults. One hundred forty-seven people visited the science exhibit in all. How would you determine how many of the visitors were adults?

    Ⓐ 63 + 147 = n
    Ⓑ 147 ÷ 63 = n
    Ⓒ 147 ÷ n = 63
    Ⓓ 63 + n = 147

7. Donald bought a rope that was 89 feet long. To divide his rope into 11 foot long sections, he solved the following problem: 89 ÷ 11 = n. How many feet of rope was left over?

    Ⓐ 0 feet
    Ⓑ 1 foot
    Ⓒ 2 feet
    Ⓓ 3 feet

8. If 976 - n = 325 is true, which of the following equations is NOT true?

    Ⓐ 976 + 325 = n
    Ⓑ 976 - 325 = n
    Ⓒ n + 325 = 976
    Ⓓ 325 + n = 976

9. Mary has $54. Jack has n times as much money as Mary does. The total amount of money Jack has is $486. What is n?

    Ⓐ 19
    Ⓑ 29
    Ⓒ 9
    Ⓓ None of these

10. Mrs. Williams went to Toys R' US to purchase the following items for each of her 3 children: one bicycle for $150, one bicycle helmet for $8, one arts and crafts set for $34 and one box of washable markers for $2 for each child. What is the total amount she spent before taxes?

    Ⓐ $194.00
    Ⓑ $582.00
    Ⓒ $572.00
    Ⓓ $482.00

11. Write an equation to show how many crayons are below.

___ × ___ = ___ crayons

12. Alice has 5 bags with 8 pens in each. Which of the following choices represent a number sentence for this situation. Note that more than one option may be correct. Select all the correct answers.

Ⓐ 8 + 8 + 8 + 8 + 8 = 40
Ⓑ 5 x 8 = 40
Ⓒ 5 + 8 = 13
Ⓓ 8 x 8 = 64

13. Create an equation from the following situation: Tim had a box of chocolates. He started with 18 chocolates, but then gave 6 to his friends. How many does he have left?

14. John draws a regular hexagon. Each side measures 12 centimeters. He also draws a rhombus. The perimeter of the hexagon and the rhombus are the same. How much does each side of the rhombus measure? Shade the cells to indicate the correct answer. Note : Each shaded cell is equivalent to 2 cms.

15. Jose purchased 4 books and 8 pens. Each book costs $3, and each pen costs $5. If he gave $100 to the shopkeeper, how much change did he receive back? Circle the correct answer.

Ⓐ $52
Ⓑ $48
Ⓒ $62
Ⓓ $38

Chapter 2

Lesson 2: Real World Problems

You can scan the QR code given below or use the url to access additional EdSearch resources including videos and mobile apps related to *Real World Problems*.

 **Real World Problems**

URL	QR Code
http://www.lumoslearning.com/a/4oaa2	

1. **There are four boxes of pears. Each box has 24 pears. How many pears are there in total?**

    Ⓐ 72 pears
    Ⓑ 48 pears
    Ⓒ 96 pears
    Ⓓ 88 pears

2. **Trevor has a collection of 450 baseball cards. He wants to place them into an album. He can fit 15 baseball cards on each page. How can Trevor figure out how many pages he will need to fit into an album all of his cards?**

    Ⓐ By adding 450 and 15
    Ⓑ By subtracting 15 from 450
    Ⓒ By multiplying 450 by 15
    Ⓓ By dividing 450 by 15

3. **Bow Wow Pet Shop has 12 dogs. Each dog had 4 puppies. How many puppies does the shop have in all?**

    Ⓐ 16 puppies
    Ⓑ 12 puppies
    Ⓒ 48 puppies
    Ⓓ 36 puppies

4. **Markers are sold in packs of 18 and 24. Yolanda bought five of the smaller packs and ten of the larger packs. How many markers did she buy altogether?**

    Ⓐ 42 markers
    Ⓑ 432 markers
    Ⓒ 320 markers
    Ⓓ 330 markers

5. **Each box of cookies contains 48 cookies. About how many cookies would be in 18 boxes?**

    Ⓐ 100 cookies
    Ⓑ 500 cookies
    Ⓒ 1,000 cookies
    Ⓓ 2,000 cookies

6. **At RTA Elementary School, there are 16 more female teachers than male teachers. If there are 60 female teachers, how can you find the number of male teachers in the school?**

     Ⓐ Subtract 16 from 60
     Ⓑ Multiply 16 by 60
     Ⓒ Add 16 to 60
     Ⓓ Divide 60 by 16

7. **Mrs. Willis wants to purchase enough Christmas ornaments so that every student can decorate 3 each. She has 24 students in her class. How many Christmas ornaments does she need to buy?**

     Ⓐ 56
     Ⓑ 72
     Ⓒ 62
     Ⓓ 58

8. **Jane needs to sell 69 cookie boxes for her scout troop. She has already sold 36 cookie boxes. How many more cookie boxes does she need to sell ?**

     Ⓐ She needs to sell 36 more boxes.
     Ⓑ She needs to sell 39 more boxes.
     Ⓒ She needs to sell 33 more boxes.
     Ⓓ She needs to sell 69 more boxes.

9. **RTA Elementary School had a 3-day food drive. On Monday, the school collected 10 soup cans and 16 cereal boxes. On Tuesday, the school collected 23 soup cans and 32 cereal boxes. On Wednesday, the school collected 36 soup cans and 44 cereal boxes. How many cereal boxes did the school collect in all?**

     Ⓐ 76 cereal boxes
     Ⓑ 92 cereal boxes
     Ⓒ 161 cereal boxes
     Ⓓ 69 cereal boxes

10. **There are 546 students in Hope School and 782 students in Trent School. How many more students are in Trent School than in Hope School?**

     Ⓐ 136 students
     Ⓑ 236 students
     Ⓒ 144 students
     Ⓓ 244 students

LumosLearning.com

11. Luke has two bags of pennies. The first bag has 8 pennies and the second bag has 6 times as many pennies as the first bag. How many pennies are in the second bag? Match each number to the correct name by darkening the circle.

	Multiplier	Number in original set	Number in second bag
48	○	○	○
8	○	○	○
6	○	○	○

12. Lisa invented a machine that would triple the number of pencils. A group of friends went to try it out, each having a different number of pencils to start.
    Fill in the table below using the rule of tripling the number of pencils

	Starting # of pencil	Multiplier	Expression	Final # of pencil
Lee	2	3		
Timmy		3	3x3	
Katie	4		4x3	
Julia	6	3	6x3	
Isabel		3		27

13. Tommy's fish tank had 8 gallons of water. He wanted to clean it so he drained 7 gallons. Once Tommy was finished, he added 9 times the amount that was in the tank. Shade the cells to show the total amount of water in the tank.
    Note: One shaded cell is equivalent to 2 gallons of water in the fish tank.

14. Charlie has $938. He wants to buy gifts for his 15 family members. He wants to spend the same amount of money (in dollars) for each person. With the remaining money, he buys a pen worth $3. How much money will he have left over after his purchases? Write your answer in the box below.

$ _____

Chapter 2

Lesson 3: Multi-Step Problems

You can scan the QR code given below or use the url to access additional EdSearch resources including videos and mobile apps related to *Multi-Step Problems*.

 Multi-Step Problems

URL	QR Code
http://www.lumoslearning.com/a/4oaa3	

1. Kristian purchased four textbooks which cost $34.99 each, and a backpack that cost $19.98. Estimate the total cost of the items he purchased. (You do not need to consider tax.)

    Ⓐ $90.00
    Ⓑ $160.00
    Ⓒ $120.00
    Ⓓ $55.00

2. During the last three games of the season, the attendance at the Tigers' home games was 14,667; 16,992; and 18,124. Estimate the total attendance for these three games. Round to the nearest thousand.

    Ⓐ 60,000
    Ⓑ 45,000
    Ⓒ 50,000
    Ⓓ 47,000

3. Steven keeps his baseball cards in an album. He has filled 147 pages of the album. He can fit 9 cards on each page. Which of the following statements is true?

    Ⓐ Steven has more than 2,000 baseball cards.
    Ⓑ Steven has between 1,000 and 1,500 baseball cards.
    Ⓒ Steven has between 1,500 and 2,000 baseball cards.
    Ⓓ Steven has less than 1,000 baseball cards.

4. Jam jars can be packed in large boxes of 60 or small boxes of 25. There are 700 jam jars to be shipped. The supplier wants to use the least number of boxes possible, but the boxes cannot be only partially filled. How many large boxes will the supplier end up using?

    Ⓐ 10 large boxes
    Ⓑ 11 large boxes
    Ⓒ 12 large boxes
    Ⓓ It is not possible to ship all 700 jars.

5. Allison needs 400 feet of rope to put a border around her yard. She can buy the rope in lengths of 36 feet. How many 36 foot long ropes will she need to buy?

    Ⓐ 9 ropes
    Ⓑ 10 ropes
    Ⓒ 11 ropes
    Ⓓ 12 ropes.

6. Katie and her friend went to the county fair. They each brought a $20.00 bill. The admission fee was $4.00 per person. Ride tickets cost 50 cents each. If each ride required two tickets per person, how many rides was each girl able to go on?

   Ⓐ 16 rides
   Ⓑ 32 rides
   Ⓒ 8 rides
   Ⓓ 20 rides

7. The population of the Bahamas is 276,208. The population of Barbados is 263,584. Which of the following statements is true of the total population of these two places?

   Ⓐ It is less than 500,000.
   Ⓑ It is between 500,000 and 550,000.
   Ⓒ It is between 550,000 and 600,000.
   Ⓓ It is more than 600,000.

8. Corey hopes to have 500 rocks in his collection by his next birthday. So far he has two boxes with 75 rocks each, a box with 85 rocks, and two boxes with 65 rocks each. How many more rocks does Corey need to gather to meet his goal?

   Ⓐ 145 rocks
   Ⓑ 135 rocks
   Ⓒ 275 rocks
   Ⓓ 235 rocks

9. Keith is helping his grandmother roll quarters to take to the bank. Each roll can hold 40 quarters. Keith's grandmother has told Keith that he can keep any leftover quarters, once the rolling is done. If there are 942 quarters to be rolled, how much money will Keith get to keep?

   Ⓐ $4.50
   Ⓑ $5.50
   Ⓒ $5.75
   Ⓓ $3.00

10. Assuming you are working with whole numbers, which of the following is not possible?

   Ⓐ Two numbers have a sum of 18 and a product of 72.
   Ⓑ Two numbers have a sum of 25 and a product of 100.
   Ⓒ Two numbers have a sum of 19 and a product of 96.
   Ⓓ Two numbers have a sum of 25 and a product of 144.

11. George and Michael are both in fourth grade, but attend different schools. George goes to Hillside Elementary and Michael goes to Sunnyside Elementary. Hillside has 7 fourth grade classes with 18 students in each class. Sunnyside has 5 fourth grade classes with 21 students in each class. Mark which of the following are correct responses.

Ⓐ Hillside has 126 fourth grade students.
Ⓑ Sunnyside has 100 fourth grade students.
Ⓒ Sunnyside has fewer fourth grade students than Hillside.
Ⓓ There are 21 more students at Hillside than Sunnyside.
Ⓔ There are 26 more students at Hillside than Sunnyside.

12. Charlie sells paintings. He charges 35 dollars for a large painting and m dollars for a small painting. He sold 8 large paintings and 6 small paintings and earned $412. How much did he charge for each small painting? Write your answer in the box below.

13. Solve each of the problems and match it with the correct answer.

	$9	$20	$10
Karen spent $122 on Christmas presents at the mall and $118 buying presents online. He gave presents to twelve of his family members. He spent the same amount of money on each of them. How much money did he spend for each member of the family?	○	○	○
Jose purchased 12 books and 9 pens. Each book costs $6, and each pen costs $2. If he gave $100 to the shopkeeper, how much change did he receive back?	○	○	○
John bought 25 pens. Each pen costs $8. He sold 15 pens at the rate of $10 per pen. At what rate (selling price per pen) did he sell the rest of them, if he made a profit of $40?	○	○	○

Chapter 2

Lesson 4: Number Theory

You can scan the QR code given below or use the url to access additional EdSearch resources including videos and mobile apps related to *Number Theory*.

ed Search	**Number Theory**	
URL		**QR Code**
http://www.lumoslearning.com/a/4oab4		

1. Andrew has a chart containing the numbers 1 through 100. He is going to put an "X" on all of the multiples of 10 and a circle around all of the multiples of 4. How many numbers will have an "X", but will not be circled?

   Ⓐ 3
   Ⓑ 4
   Ⓒ 5
   Ⓓ 8

2. Which number is a multiple of 30?

   Ⓐ 3
   Ⓑ 6
   Ⓒ 60
   Ⓓ 50

3. Use the Venn diagram below to respond to the following question.

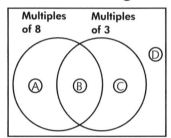

   In which region of the diagram would the number 72 be found?

   Ⓐ Region A
   Ⓑ Region B
   Ⓒ Region C
   Ⓓ Region D

4. Which number can divide 28 evenly?

   Ⓐ 3
   Ⓑ 6
   Ⓒ 7
   Ⓓ 5

5. Use the Venn diagram below to respond to the following question. Which of the following numbers would be found in Region D?

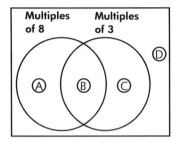

Ⓐ 41
Ⓑ 53
Ⓒ 62
Ⓓ All of the above

6. Which of these sets contains no composite numbers?

Ⓐ 97, 71, 59, 29
Ⓑ 256, 155, 75, 15
Ⓒ 5, 23, 87, 91
Ⓓ 2, 11, 19, 51

7. Choose the set that consists of only prime numbers.

Ⓐ 2, 4, 8, 12
Ⓑ 13, 15, 17, 19
Ⓒ 2, 5, 23, 29
Ⓓ 3, 17, 29, 81

8. Which of the following sets include factors of 44?

Ⓐ 2, 4, 11, 22
Ⓑ 0, 2, 6, 11
Ⓒ 2, 4, 12, 22
Ⓓ 4, 8, 12, 22

9. Which number completes the following number sentences?
$72 ÷ \_\_\_ = 6$
$\_\_\_ × 6 = 72$

Ⓐ 6
Ⓑ 8
Ⓒ 12
Ⓓ 16

10. If Carla wants to complete exactly 63 push ups during her workout, it is best if she does her push-ups in sets of _____.

Ⓐ 13
Ⓑ 8
Ⓒ 7
Ⓓ 17

11. Read each number below and mark whether it is a factor of 24, 30, or both.

	Factor of 24	Factor of 30	Factor of 30 and 24
2	○	○	○
3	○	○	○
5	○	○	○
8	○	○	○
10	○	○	○
12	○	○	○

12. Identify the prime number and write it in the box given below:

13, 15, 9, 100, 28, 77

13. Circle all the factors of 24

1	2	3	4
5	6	7	8
9	10	11	12
13	14	15	16
17	18	19	20
21	22	23	24

14. **Charlie has a chart containing the numbers 1 through 100. He is going to put an "X" on all of the multiples of 6 and a circle around all of the multiples of 8. Which of the following statements are correct? Choose all the correct answers.**

Ⓐ 12 numbers are circled.

Ⓑ 9 numbers are circled but do not have X on them.

Ⓒ 4 numbers are circled and also have X on them.

Ⓓ 12 numbers have X on them but are not circled.

Chapter 2

Lesson 5: Patterns

You can scan the QR code given below or use the url to access additional EdSearch resources including videos and mobile apps related to *Patterns*.

 **Patterns**

URL	QR Code
http://www.lumoslearning.com/a/4oa5	

1. Which of the following is NOT a true statement about the number sequence below?
   26, 39, 52, 65, 78, 91

   Ⓐ The numbers are decreasing by 13.
   Ⓑ The sequence contains both even and odd numbers.
   Ⓒ The numbers are increasing by 13.
   Ⓓ The numbers are all multiples of 13.

2. What would be the next three numbers in this pattern?
   14, 21, 28, 35,

   Ⓐ 42, 50, 58
   Ⓑ 42, 49, 56
   Ⓒ 42, 49, 58
   Ⓓ 42, 48, 54

3. Which of the following is NOT true of this pattern?
   125,000; 150,000; 175,000; 200,000; 225,000

   Ⓐ The numbers are not descending.
   Ⓑ The numbers are all even.
   Ⓒ The numbers are increasing by 25,000.
   Ⓓ The numbers are all multiples of 50,000.

4. What is the missing number in this pattern?
   24, 36, ___, 60, 72

   Ⓐ 50
   Ⓑ 54
   Ⓒ 48
   Ⓓ 46

5. Study the following pattern. Then find the next two terms.
   0, 10, 8, 18, 16, 26, 24, ___, ___

   Ⓐ 36, 34
   Ⓑ 34, 44
   Ⓒ 32, 30
   Ⓓ 34, 32

LumosLearning.com

6. Darren was skip-counting by 5's starting from 2. He said, "2, 7, 12, 17, . . ." After a while, he noticed a pattern in the numbers. Based on the pattern, which of the following numbers will Darren eventually say?

   Ⓐ 720
   Ⓑ 275
   Ⓒ 187
   Ⓓ 271

7. Assume this pattern continues. Which number would not be part of the sequence?
   12, 24, 36, 48, 60, . . .

   Ⓐ 112
   Ⓑ 108
   Ⓒ 120
   Ⓓ 96

8. What is the rule in the following pattern?
   8, 12, 16, 20, 24, 28

   Ⓐ add 4
   Ⓑ subtract 8
   Ⓒ add 3
   Ⓓ add 6

9. Warren likes to eat spoonfuls of dried strawberries out of his bowl of cereal. His bowl has 20 of them. He can fit 5 strawberries on the spoon at one time. How many are still left in the bowl after the third spoonful?

   Ⓐ 15 strawberries
   Ⓑ 5 strawberries
   Ⓒ 10 strawberries
   Ⓓ 1 strawberry

10. Larry produced exactly 12 clown wigs in an 8 hour day, for 3 days. Which pattern shows how many clown wigs were made in 5 weeks?

   Ⓐ 3, 8, 12; 3, 8, 12; 3, 8, 12; 3, 8, 12; 3, 8, 12
   Ⓑ 3, 8, 12; 3, 8, 13; 3, 8, 14; 3, 8, 15; 3, 8, 16
   Ⓒ 3, 8, 12; 3, 8, 24; 3, 8, 36; 3, 8, 48; 3, 8, 60
   Ⓓ 3, 8, 12; 3, 8, 144; 3, 8, 1728; 3, 8, 17,726

11. Select the shape that completes the pattern

	▭	☐	○	△
▭ ○ ☐ ▭	○	○	○	○
△ ○ △ ○ △ ○	○	○	○	○
☐ △ ○ ▭ ▭ ○	○	○	○	○
○ ▭ ☐ △ ○ ▭	○	○	○	○

12. Fill in the missing boxes in the table to complete each pattern or sequence of numbers Start from the left side of the table to complete the sequence.

1		3	4		6
2	4		8	10	
	12	18		30	36
10		18	22	26	

13. Find the rule for this IN-OUT table. Circle the correct answer choice

IN	OUT
72	8
63	7
45	5

Ⓐ Divide by 8
Ⓑ Subtract by 56
Ⓒ Subtract by64
Ⓓ Divide by 9

14. Determine the rule for this table. Then use the rule to answer the following question.
    What number will come out when the **IN** value is 25? Enter your answer in the blank box.

IN	OUT
12	8
15	11
20	16
25	

15. Assume this pattern continues. Which numbers would be part of the sequence? Note that
    more than one option may be correct.
    84, 91, 98, 105 .....
    Select all the correct answers.

Ⓐ 343
Ⓑ 288
Ⓒ 245
Ⓓ 167

End of Operations and Algebraic Thinking

Chapter 3:
Number & Operations in Base Ten

Lesson 1: Place Value

You can scan the QR code given below or use the url to access additional EdSearch resources including videos and mobile apps related to *Place Value*.

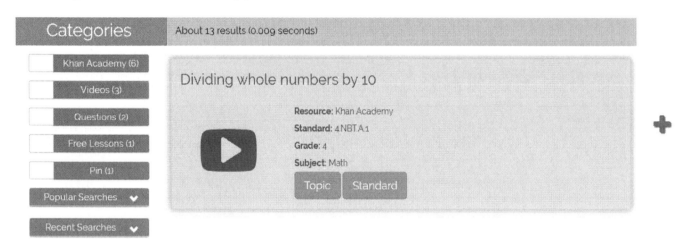

Categories	About 13 results (0.009 seconds)
Khan Academy (6)	**Dividing whole numbers by 10**
Videos (3)	
Questions (2)	**Resource:** Khan Academy
Free Lessons (1)	**Standard:** 4.NBT.A.1
Pin (1)	**Grade:** 4
Popular Searches ⌄	**Subject:** Math
Recent Searches ⌄	Topic Standard

ed Search   *Place Value*

URL	QR Code
http://www.lumoslearning.com/a/4nbta1	

Name _____   Date _____

1. What number can be found in the ten-thousands digit of 291,807?

    Ⓐ 9
    Ⓑ 1
    Ⓒ 2
    Ⓓ 0

2. Consider the number 890,260.
    The 8 is found in the _____ place.

    Ⓐ ten-thousands
    Ⓑ millions
    Ⓒ thousands
    Ⓓ hundred-thousands

Place Value Chart

Hundred-billions	Ten-billions	Billions	Hundred-millions	Ten-millions	Millions	Hundred-thousands	Ten-thousands	Thousands	Hundreds	Tens	Ones

3. What number correctly completes this statement?
    9 ten thousands = _____ thousands

    Ⓐ 90
    Ⓑ 900
    Ⓒ 9
    Ⓓ 19

4. **Which number is in the thousands place in the number 984,923?**

   Ⓐ 9
   Ⓑ 8
   Ⓒ 4
   Ⓓ 2

5. **What is the value of the 8 in 683,345?**

   Ⓐ 80
   Ⓑ 800
   Ⓒ 8,000
   Ⓓ 80,000

6. **Which number equals 4 thousands, 6 hundreds, 0 tens, and 5 ones?**

   Ⓐ 465
   Ⓑ 4,605
   Ⓒ 4,650
   Ⓓ 4,065

7. **What number is in the tens place in 156.25?**

   Ⓐ 1
   Ⓑ 5
   Ⓒ 6
   Ⓓ 2

8. **Which number equals 2 ten thousands, 1 hundred thousand, and 3 ones**

   Ⓐ 120,003
   Ⓑ 210,003
   Ⓒ 102,003
   Ⓓ 213,000

9. **Which answer shows the value of each 7 in this number: 7,777?**

   Ⓐ 7,000, 700, 70, 7
   Ⓑ 7 x 7 x 7 x 7
   Ⓒ 700,000, 70,000, 700, 70
   Ⓓ 7 + 7 + 7 + 7

10. Mrs. Winters went to the bank with eight 100 dollar bills. She wanted to replace them with all 10 dollar bills. How many 10 dollar bills will the bank give her in exchange?

Ⓐ 800 ten dollar bills
Ⓑ 8,000 ten dollar bills
Ⓒ 8 ten dollar bills
Ⓓ 80 ten dollar bills

11. **Select the correct value for each number**

	5	50	500
How many hundreds are in 500?	○	○	○
How many tens are in 500?	○	○	○
How many ones are in 500?	○	○	○

12. **Select the correct value for each number**

	9	90	900
How many hundreds are in 900?	○	○	○
How many tens are in 900?	○	○	○
How many ones are in 900?	○	○	○

13. **Which number equals 8 millions, 5 tens? Circle the correct answer**

Ⓐ   800,050
Ⓑ   8,000,500
Ⓒ   8,000,005
Ⓓ   8,000,050

14. **John has $500. Karen has 10 times as much money. How much money does Karen have? Write your answer in the box below**

(_____)

Chapter 3

Lesson 2: Compare Numbers and Expanded Notation

You can scan the QR code given below or use the url to access additional EdSearch resources including videos and mobile apps related to *Compare Numbers and Expanded Notation*.

 **Compare Numbers and Expanded Notation**

URL	QR Code
http://www.lumoslearning.com/a/4nbta2	

1. **Arrange the following numbers in ascending order.**
    62,894; 26,894; 26,849; 62,984

    A 62,984; 62,894; 26,894; 26,849
    B 26,894; 26,849; 62,984; 62,894
    C 26,849; 62,984; 62,894; 26,894
    D 26,849; 26,894; 62,894; 62,984

2. **Which of the following statements is true?**

    A 189,624 > 189,898
    B 189,624 > 189,246
    C 189,624 < 189,264
    D 189,624 = 189,462

3. **Which number will make this statement true?**
    198,888 > _____

    A 198,898
    B 198,879
    C 198,889
    D 199,888

4. **Which statement is NOT true?**

    A 798 < 799
    B 798 > 789
    C 798 < 789
    D 798 = 798

5. **Write the expanded form of this number.**
    954,351

    A 90,000 + 5,000 + 400 + 30 + 5 + 1
    B 900,000 + 50,000 + 4,000 + 300 + 50 + 1
    C 900,000 + 54,000 + 300 + 50 + 1
    D 900,000 + 50,000 + 4,000 + 300 + 51

6. **What is the standard form of this number?**
   30,000 + 200 + 50

   Ⓐ 30,250
   Ⓑ 32,500
   Ⓒ 325,000
   Ⓓ 3,250

7. **Write the standard form of:**
   8 ten thousands, 4 thousands, 1 hundred, 6 ones

   Ⓐ 84,160
   Ⓑ 84,106
   Ⓒ 8,416
   Ⓓ 84,016

8. **Write 1,975,206 in expanded form.**

   Ⓐ 1,000,000 + 9,000,000 + 7,000 + 500 + 20 + 6
   Ⓑ 1,000,000 + 9,000,000 + 70,000 + 5,000 + 200 + 60
   Ⓒ 100,000 + 900,000 + 70,000 + 5,000 + 200 + 6
   Ⓓ 1,000,000 + 900,000 + 70,000 + 5,000 + 200 + 6

9. **What is 300,000 + 40,000 + 20 + 5 in standard form?**

   Ⓐ 34,025
   Ⓑ 3,425
   Ⓒ 340,025
   Ⓓ 342,005

10. **Write the standard form for 2 hundred thousands, 1 ten thousand, 4 hundreds, 1 ten, 9 ones.**

    Ⓐ 210,419
    Ⓑ 201,419
    Ⓒ 200,419
    Ⓓ 21,419

11. Compare the numbers then select <, >, or = to make the sentence true.

	<	>	=
4,145 ___ 4,451	○	○	○
31,600 __ 63,100	○	○	○
49 _____ 49	○	○	○
831 _____ 381	○	○	○

12. Write the standard form of the number shown below in the given box with a comma in the correct place.

2,000 + 500 + 9

13. Compare the numbers then select <, >, or = to make the sentence true.

	<	>	=
124 __ 789	○	○	○
12,947 __ 19,247	○	○	○
412 __ 412	○	○	○
94,811 __ 81,944	○	○	○

14. The number of toothpicks produced each day in a factory is given below.

Toothpicks Produced	
Day	Number of Toothpicks Produced
Monday	825,347
Tuesday	825,374
Wednesday	825,743
Thursday	852,743
Friday	852,743

On which day did the factory produce the least number of toothpicks? Mark the correct answer.

Ⓐ Monday
Ⓑ Tuesday
Ⓒ Wednesday
Ⓓ Thursday

Chapter 3

Lesson 3: Rounding Numbers

You can scan the QR code given below or use the url to access additional EdSearch resources including videos and mobile apps related to *Rounding Numbers*.

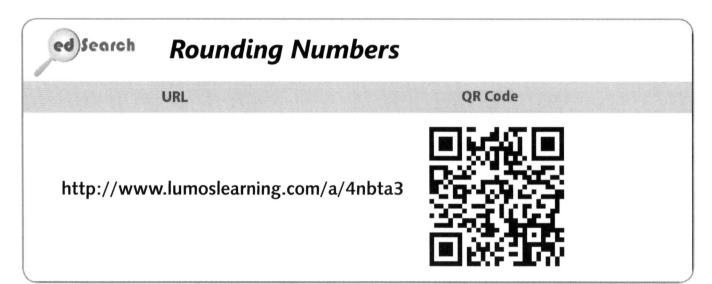

ed Search

Rounding Numbers

URL	QR Code
http://www.lumoslearning.com/a/4nbta3	

1. **Round 4,170,154 to the nearest hundred.**

   Ⓐ 4,200,000
   Ⓑ 4,170,100
   Ⓒ 4,170,000
   Ⓓ 4,170,200

2. **Round 4,170,154 to the nearest thousand.**

   Ⓐ 4,200,000
   Ⓑ 180,000
   Ⓒ 4,170,000
   Ⓓ 4,179,200

3. **Round 4,170,154 to the nearest ten thousand.**

   Ⓐ 4,200,000
   Ⓑ 4,170,000
   Ⓒ 4,179,000
   Ⓓ 4,179,200

4. **Round 4,170,154 to the nearest hundred thousand.**

   Ⓐ 4,200,000
   Ⓑ 4,180,000
   Ⓒ 4,179,000
   Ⓓ 4,100,000

5. **Round 4,170,154 to the nearest million.**

   Ⓐ 4,000,000
   Ⓑ 4,180,000
   Ⓒ 4,179,000
   Ⓓ 5,000,000

6. **Round 424,819 to the nearest ten.**

   Ⓐ 400,820
   Ⓑ 424,810
   Ⓒ 424,020
   Ⓓ 424,820

7. The soda factory bottles 2,451 grape and 3,092 orange sodas each day. About how many of the two types of soda are bottled each day? Round the numbers to the nearest hundred and add them.

    Ⓐ 5,400 sodas
    Ⓑ 5,000 sodas
    Ⓒ 5,600 sodas
    Ⓓ 5,500 sodas

8. The Campbells have 3,000 books in their personal library. If 1,479 of the books are fiction, and the rest are non-fiction. How many are non-fiction? Round to the nearest hundred.

    Ⓐ 2,500 books
    Ⓑ 1,400 books
    Ⓒ 1,500 books
    Ⓓ 1,600 books

9. Solve; Give an estimate as the final answer.
    7000 - 4258 = ?

    Ⓐ 2,600
    Ⓑ 3,000
    Ⓒ 2,000
    Ⓓ 6,858

10. The school has $925 to spend on new books for the library. Each book costs $9.95. Estimate how many books can be bought.

    Ⓐ 70
    Ⓑ 80
    Ⓒ 90
    Ⓓ 120

11. **Match each statement with the way in which it is rounded.**

	Nearest 10	Nearest 100	Nearest 1,000	Nearest 10,000
4,893 rounded to 4,890	○	○	○	○
15,309 rounded to 20,000	○	○	○	○
32,350 rounded to 32,000	○	○	○	○
523 rounded to 500	○	○	○	○

12. **Round 14,623 to the nearest hundred.**

(_____)

13. **Match each statement with the way in which it is rounded**

	Nearest 10	Nearest 100	Nearest 1,000	Nearest 10,000
19,989 rounded to 19,990	○	○	○	○
86,415 rounded to 90,000	○	○	○	○
909 rounded to 1,000	○	○	○	○
8,525 rounded to 8,500	○	○	○	○

14. **If the number 750,025 is rounded to the nearest then thousand to get 760,000, What would be the list of possible digits that could go in the thousands place? Circle the correct answer.**

Ⓐ 5,6,7,8,9
Ⓑ 6,7,8,9
Ⓒ 0,1,2,3,4
Ⓓ 0,1,2,3,4,5

Chapter 3

Lesson 4: Addition & Subtraction

You can scan the QR code given below or use the url to access additional EdSearch resources including videos and mobile apps related to *Addition & Subtraction*.

 **Addition & Subtraction**

URL	QR Code
http://www.lumoslearning.com/a/4nbtb4	

1. **What number acts as the identity element in addition?**

    Ⓐ -1
    Ⓑ 0
    Ⓒ 1
    Ⓓ None of these

2. **Which of the following number sentences illustrates the Commutative Property of Addition?**

    Ⓐ 3 + 7 = 7 + 3
    Ⓑ 9 + 4 = 10 + 3
    Ⓒ 11 + 0 = 11
    Ⓓ 2 + (3 + 4) = 2 + 7

3. **What number makes this number sentence true?**
    10 + ___ = 0

    Ⓐ 10
    Ⓑ $\frac{4}{10}$
    Ⓒ 0
    Ⓓ -10

4. **Find the sum.**
    24 + 37 + 76 + 13

    Ⓐ 140
    Ⓑ 150
    Ⓒ 151
    Ⓓ none of these

5. **Find the difference.**
    702 - 314 = ____

    Ⓐ 388
    Ⓑ 412
    Ⓒ 312
    Ⓓ 402

6. **What is the sum of 0.55 + 6.35?**

   Ⓐ 6.09
   Ⓑ 0.85
   Ⓒ 6.90
   Ⓓ none of these

7. **Find the difference.**
   7.86 - 4.88

   Ⓐ 2.98
   Ⓑ 3.02
   Ⓒ 2.08
   Ⓓ 1.98

8. **Find the sum.**
   156 + 99 =

   Ⓐ 256
   Ⓑ 245
   Ⓒ 265
   Ⓓ 255

9. **There are 1,565 pictures on the disks. Only 1,430 of them are in color. How many pictures are not in color?**

   Ⓐ 135 pictures
   Ⓑ 2,995 pictures
   Ⓒ 2,195 pictures
   Ⓓ 995 pictures

10. **James got 300 coins while diving in the game, The Amazing World of Gumball Splashmasters! However, he hit 2 birds and lost 12 coins. During the second round, he got 250 coins and hit no birds. How many coins did he have at the end of the second round?**

    Ⓐ 500 coins
    Ⓑ 542 coins
    Ⓒ 548 coins
    Ⓓ 538 coins

11. Select all of the following expressions that will equal 4,189

Ⓐ 4,002 + 187
Ⓑ 6,100 – 2,189
Ⓒ 12,555 – 8,366
Ⓓ 859 + 3,985

12. Fill in the missing number that will make the addition problem true.

```
  1525
+2_98
 3923
```

13. Enter the missing number that will make the subtraction problem true.

```
  7598
-2_98
 5500
```

14. Find the sum: 4,927 + 5,098. Circle the correct answer.

Ⓐ 9025
Ⓑ 9925
Ⓒ 10,025
Ⓓ 10,015

Chapter 3

Lesson 5: Multiplication

You can scan the QR code given below or use the url to access additional EdSearch resources including videos and mobile apps related to *Multiplication*.

ed Search	**Multiplication**	
URL		**QR Code**
http://www.lumoslearning.com/a/4nbtb5		

1. Assume a function table has the rule "Multiply by 6." What would the OUT value be if the IN value was 8?

    Ⓐ 14
    Ⓑ 48
    Ⓒ 16
    Ⓓ 32

2. Solve.
    26 x 8 = ___

    Ⓐ 206
    Ⓑ 168
    Ⓒ 182
    Ⓓ 208

3. The number sentence 4 x 1 = 4 illustrates which mathematical property?

    Ⓐ The Associative Property of Multiplication
    Ⓑ The Identity Property of Multiplication
    Ⓒ The Distributive Property
    Ⓓ The Associative Property of Multiplication

4. Find the product of 17 x 6.

    Ⓐ 102
    Ⓑ 84
    Ⓒ 119
    Ⓓ 153

5. If the IN value is 0, what is the OUT value?

    RULE: Divide by 9

IN	OUT
0	??
9	1
81	9
99	11

    Ⓐ 2
    Ⓑ 0
    Ⓒ 9
    Ⓓ 1

6. **Which of the following number sentences illustrates the Associative Property of Multiplication?**

    Ⓐ 4 x 0 = 0
    Ⓑ 77 x 1 = 1 x 77
    Ⓒ (2 x 4) x 5 = 2 x (4 x 5)
    Ⓓ 13 x 7 = (10 x 7) + (3 x 7)

7. **Solve.**
    4 x 3 x 6 = _____

    Ⓐ 48
    Ⓑ 72
    Ⓒ 56
    Ⓓ 64

8. **Find the exact product of 5 x 20 x 8.**

    Ⓐ 800
    Ⓑ 560
    Ⓒ 80
    Ⓓ 900

9. **Complete the following statement:**
    "In a multiplication sentence, if a factor is 1, then _____ "

    Ⓐ the other factor is also 1
    Ⓑ the product is also 1
    Ⓒ the other factor and the product are the same
    Ⓓ the product is 0

10. **Steve has 7 pages in his stamp collection book. Each page holds 20 stamps. How many total stamps does Steve have in his collection?**

    Ⓐ 14
    Ⓑ 6
    Ⓒ 140
    Ⓓ 8

11. Select the correct statement for each multiplication fact.

	True	False
75 x 5 = 375	◯	◯
28 x 12 = 334	◯	◯
72 x 9 = 648	◯	◯
45 x 21 = 945	◯	◯

12. Fill in the correct numbers to complete each multiplication sentence.

5	x	▭	=	65
23	x	14	=	▭
▭	x	34	=	340
52	x	▭	=	104

13. Circle the correct answer to the multiplication problem 14 x 12.

Ⓐ 140
Ⓑ 168
Ⓒ 186
Ⓓ 120

14. The van traveled 1,458 miles every day from Monday through Friday. How many miles did it travel in all? Write your answer in the box below.

⬭

Chapter 3

Lesson 6: Division

You can scan the QR code given below or use the url to access additional EdSearch resources including videos and mobile apps related to *Division*.

ed)Search **Division**	
URL	**QR Code**
http://www.lumoslearning.com/a/4nbtb5	

1. **What role does the number 75 play in the following equation?**
   $300 \div 75 = 4$

   Ⓐ It is the dividend.
   Ⓑ It is the quotient.
   Ⓒ It is the divisor.
   Ⓓ It is the remainder.

2. **Which of the following division expressions will have no remainder?**

   Ⓐ $73 \div 9$
   Ⓑ $82 \div 6$
   Ⓒ $91 \div 7$
   Ⓓ $39 \div 9$

3. **Divide these blocks into 2 equal groups. How many will be in each group?**
   Note: 1 flat = 10 rods. 1 rod = 10 cubes

   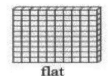 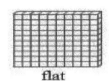

   flat   flat   flat   rods   cubes

   Ⓐ 352
   Ⓑ 176
   Ⓒ 152
   Ⓓ 132

4. **Fill in the blank:**
   $480 \div 6 = (400 \div 6) + (80 \div \_\_\_)$

   Ⓐ 400
   Ⓑ 6
   Ⓒ 80
   Ⓓ 480

5. **What amount would be in each group if this number were divided into 6 groups?**
   Note: 1 flat = 10 rods. 1 rod = 10 cubes

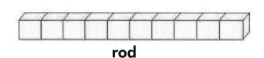

flat   flat   rod

Ⓐ 35
Ⓑ 45
Ⓒ 25
Ⓓ 15

6. **Find the quotient:**
   694 ÷ 2 = ____

   Ⓐ 342
   Ⓑ 327
   Ⓒ 347
   Ⓓ 332

7. **What is the remainder when 100 is divided by 12?**

   Ⓐ 4
   Ⓑ 6
   Ⓒ 8
   Ⓓ 2

8. **28 x 6 = 168**
   Find a related fact to the one shown above.

   Ⓐ 28 ÷ 16 = 8
   Ⓑ 168 ÷ 6 = 28
   Ⓒ 168 ÷ 28 = 8
   Ⓓ 168 ÷ 8 = 16

9. **Thomas took 96 bottles of spring water to the family reunion picnic. If they had purchased 4 identical cases, how many bottles were in each case?**

   Ⓐ 12
   Ⓑ 48
   Ⓒ 24
   Ⓓ 18

10. Each of Mrs. Harris' 7 children collected the same number of exotic insects for their individual displays. How many insects did each child have for show and tell, if they had a total of 112 insects?

Ⓐ 112
Ⓑ 16
Ⓒ 7
Ⓓ 42

11. Select all of the following problems that do not have remainders in their answer.

Ⓐ 28 ÷ 7
Ⓑ 16 ÷ 5
Ⓒ 17 ÷ 3
Ⓓ 42 ÷ 5

12 Fill in the blank that will make the following division sentence true.

512 ÷ ____ = 256

13. Complete the following table.

Dividend	Divisor	Quotient	Remainder
128	8	16	0
435	7		
350	6		

14. John bought 6 packs of beads. Each pack has the same number of beads. Altogether, he has 1,494 beads. How many beads are in each pack? Circle the correct answer.

Ⓐ 259 beads
Ⓑ 249 beads
Ⓒ 247 beads
Ⓓ 229 beads

End of Number and Operations in Base Ten

Chapter 4:
Number & Operations - Fractions

Lesson 1: Equivalent Fractions

You can scan the QR code given below or use the url to access additional EdSearch resources including videos and mobile apps related to *Equivalent Fractions*.

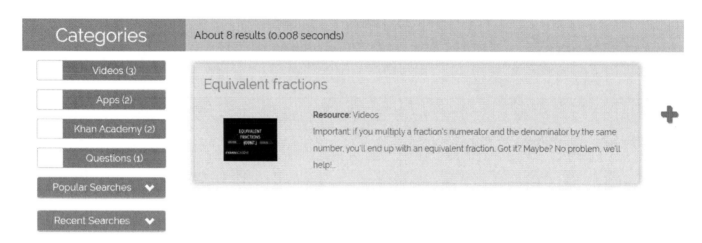

Categories

About 8 results (0.008 seconds)

Videos (3)

Apps (2)

Khan Academy (2)

Questions (1)

Popular Searches ⌄

Recent Searches ⌄

Equivalent fractions

Resource: Videos

Important: if you multiply a fraction's numerator and the denominator by the same number, you'll end up with an equivalent fraction. Got it? Maybe? No problem, we'll help!...

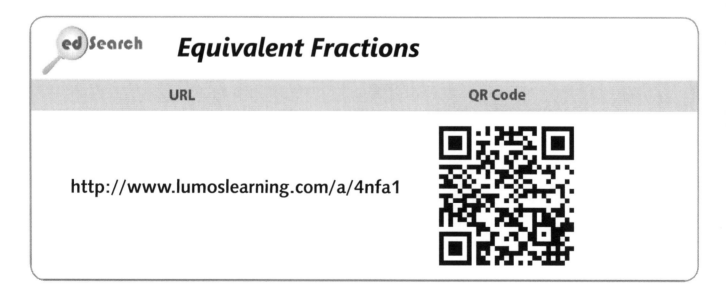

ed)Search   *Equivalent Fractions*

URL	QR Code
http://www.lumoslearning.com/a/4nfa1	

1. **What fraction of these shapes are squares?**

  ○ ● ▲

△ △ ● ■ □

Ⓐ $\frac{1}{4}$

Ⓑ $\frac{4}{6}$

Ⓒ $\frac{4}{10}$

Ⓓ $\frac{1}{3}$

2. **What fraction of these shapes are not circles?**

□ □ ○ ● ▲

△ △ ● ■ □

Ⓐ $\frac{3}{7}$

Ⓑ $\frac{8}{10}$

Ⓒ $\frac{7}{10}$

Ⓓ $\frac{1}{3}$

3. **What fraction of the squares are shaded?**

□ □ ○ ● ▲

△ △ ● ■ □

Ⓐ $\frac{1}{4}$

Ⓑ $\frac{1}{10}$

Ⓒ $\frac{1}{3}$

Ⓓ $\frac{3}{4}$

4. **What fraction of the shaded shapes are circles?**

□ □ ○ ● ▲
△ △ ● ■ □

Ⓐ $\frac{2}{10}$

Ⓑ $\frac{1}{3}$

Ⓒ $\frac{2}{2}$

Ⓓ $\frac{2}{4}$

5. **Continue the pattern of equivalent fractions:**
    $\frac{1}{2}, \frac{2}{4}, \frac{3}{6}, \frac{4}{8} \cdots$
    What fraction would come next in the pattern?

Ⓐ $\frac{1}{3}$

Ⓑ $\frac{1}{16}$

Ⓒ $\frac{5}{10}$

Ⓓ $\frac{3}{4}$

6. **Which pair of addends have the fraction $\frac{11}{12}$ as a sum?**

Ⓐ $\frac{9}{6} + \frac{2}{6}$

Ⓑ $\frac{7}{12} + \frac{4}{12}$

Ⓒ $\frac{9}{12} + \frac{1}{12}$

Ⓓ $\frac{11}{12} + \frac{1}{1}$

7. **Which fraction is equivalent to this model?**

Ⓐ $\frac{1}{5}$

Ⓑ $\frac{3}{7}$

Ⓒ $\frac{2}{7}$

Ⓓ $\frac{4}{16}$

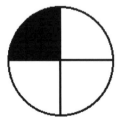

8. **Which fraction is equivalent to 8/18?**

   Ⓐ $\frac{1}{5}$

   Ⓑ $\frac{3}{7}$

   Ⓒ $\frac{2}{7}$

   Ⓓ $\frac{4}{9}$

9. **Continue the pattern of equivalent fractions:**
   $$\frac{5}{6}, \frac{10}{12}, \frac{15}{18} \cdots$$
   What fraction would come next in the pattern?

   Ⓐ $\frac{7}{14}$

   Ⓑ $\frac{20}{24}$

   Ⓒ $\frac{9}{45}$

   Ⓓ $\frac{12}{36}$

10. **Reduce the fraction $\frac{21}{49}$ to its lowest terms:**

   Ⓐ $\frac{1}{5}$

   Ⓑ $\frac{3}{7}$

   Ⓒ $\frac{2}{7}$

   Ⓓ $\frac{4}{9}$

11. **Reduce the fraction $\frac{44}{99}$ to its lowest terms:**

   Ⓐ $\frac{1}{5}$

   Ⓑ $\frac{3}{7}$

   Ⓒ $\frac{2}{7}$

   Ⓓ $\frac{4}{9}$

12. Patrick climbed $\frac{4}{5}$ of the way up the trunk of a tree. Jacob climbed $\frac{80}{100}$ of the way up the same tree. To accomplish the same distance as Patrick and Jacob, how far up that tree trunk will Devon have to climb?

Ⓐ $\frac{15}{20}$

Ⓑ $\frac{60}{75}$

Ⓒ $\frac{100}{200}$

Ⓓ $\frac{28}{42}$

13. The cheerleaders ate $\frac{9}{18}$ of a sheet cake. Write this fraction in lowest terms.

Ⓐ $\frac{1}{9}$

Ⓑ $\frac{1}{2}$

Ⓒ $\frac{2}{3}$

Ⓓ $\frac{3}{6}$

14. Which group of fractions can all be reduced to $\frac{2}{9}$?

Ⓐ $\frac{23}{27}, \frac{4}{36}, \frac{30}{270}$

Ⓑ $\frac{25}{50}, \frac{30}{60}, \frac{50}{100}$

Ⓒ $\frac{4}{18}, \frac{6}{27}, \frac{50}{225}$

Ⓓ $\frac{6}{21}, \frac{20}{70}, \frac{36}{84}$

15. What do these fractions have in common?
$\frac{10}{16}, \frac{15}{24}, \frac{20}{32}, \frac{25}{40}, \frac{30}{48}$

Ⓐ These fractions are equivalent to $\frac{5}{9}$.

Ⓑ These fractions are equivalent to $\frac{5}{8}$

Ⓒ These fractions are equivalent to $\frac{10}{12}$.

Ⓓ These fractions are equivalent to $\frac{4}{8}$.

16. Select whether the fraction pair is equivalent or not equivalent.

	Equivalent	Not Equivalent
$\frac{12}{15}$ and $\frac{3}{5}$	○	○
$\frac{18}{24}$ and $\frac{9}{12}$	○	○
$\frac{18}{200}$ and $\frac{9}{100}$	○	○
$\frac{3}{15}$ and $\frac{3}{25}$	○	○

17. Write the simplest form of $\frac{120}{150}$. Write the answer in the box given below.

18. Circle on all of the fractions that can be simplified to $\frac{1}{2}$

- Ⓐ $\frac{24}{26}$
- Ⓑ $\frac{2}{4}$
- Ⓒ $\frac{5}{11}$
- Ⓓ $\frac{35}{70}$
- Ⓔ $\frac{9}{20}$
- Ⓕ $\frac{7}{14}$

19. Which group of fractions are equivalent to $\frac{4}{12}$? Select all the correct answers.

- Ⓐ $\frac{1}{3}$, $\frac{2}{5}$, $\frac{3}{9}$
- Ⓑ $\frac{1}{3}$, $\frac{2}{6}$, $\frac{3}{9}$
- Ⓒ $\frac{1}{3}$, $\frac{2}{5}$, $\frac{5}{20}$
- Ⓓ $\frac{6}{18}$, $\frac{12}{36}$, $\frac{15}{45}$

Chapter 4

Lesson 2: Compare Fractions

You can scan the QR code given below or use the url to access additional EdSearch resources including videos and mobile apps related to *Compare Fractions*.

 **Compare Fractions**

URL	QR Code
http://www.lumoslearning.com/a/4nfa2	

1. **Where is Point D located on this number line?**

Ⓐ -2.5

Ⓑ -2

Ⓒ -1.5

Ⓓ -3

2. **Which statement is true?**

Ⓐ $\frac{4}{14} = \frac{6}{21} = \frac{8}{28}$

Ⓑ $\frac{4}{14} > \frac{6}{21} > \frac{8}{28}$

Ⓒ $\frac{4}{14} < \frac{6}{21} < \frac{8}{28}$

Ⓓ $\frac{4}{14} < \frac{6}{21} > \frac{8}{28}$

3. **Compare the two fractions using < = or >:**

$\frac{3}{12}$ _____ $\frac{3}{18}$

Ⓐ =

Ⓑ <

Ⓒ >

4. **Compare the two fractions using < = or >:**

$\frac{4}{28}$ _____ $\frac{4}{20}$

Ⓐ =

Ⓑ <

Ⓒ >

5. **Which symbol makes this statement true?**

$\frac{4}{9} + \frac{3}{9}$ ____ $\frac{6}{9}$

Ⓐ >

Ⓑ =

Ⓒ <

6. **Which symbol makes this statement true?**

$\frac{75}{100} - \frac{32}{100}$ ____ $\frac{42}{100}$

Ⓐ >

Ⓑ =

Ⓒ <

7. **Which fraction below has a greater value than the fraction being shown?**

Ⓐ $\frac{2}{20}$

Ⓑ $\frac{2}{15}$

Ⓒ $\frac{2}{10}$

Ⓓ $\frac{2}{100}$

8. **The popsicle slowly melted in the hot sun. Which group of fractions could represent the amount of popsicle remaining after 2 minutes, 4 minutes, and 6 minutes had passed?**

Ⓐ $\frac{1}{3}, \frac{1}{2}, \frac{3}{4}$

Ⓑ $\frac{3}{4}, \frac{1}{2}, \frac{1}{3}$

Ⓒ $\frac{1}{3}, \frac{3}{4}, \frac{1}{2}$

Ⓓ $\frac{3}{4}, \frac{1}{3}, \frac{1}{2}$

9. **Arrange these models in order from greatest to least:**

Model A   Model B   Model C   Model D

Ⓐ A, B, C, D

Ⓑ C, A, D, B

Ⓒ C, D, B, A

Ⓓ A, C, D, B

10. Compare the fractions using <, =, or >.

$$\frac{692}{1000} + \frac{231}{1000} \underline{\quad} \frac{245}{1000} + \frac{726}{1000}$$

    Ⓐ   <

    Ⓑ   =

    Ⓒ   >

11. These fractions are arranged from least to greatest. Which fraction could go in the blank?

$$\frac{9}{25}, \underline{\quad}, \frac{16}{25}, \frac{21}{25}$$

    Ⓐ $\frac{13}{25}$

    Ⓑ $\frac{6}{25}$

    Ⓒ $\frac{18}{25}$

    Ⓓ $\frac{23}{25}$

12. Marty eats vegetables $\frac{6}{7}$ days out of the week. Dan eats them $\frac{3}{7}$ days out of the week. How many more days does Marty eat vegetables each week?

    Ⓐ   2 days

    Ⓑ   1 day

    Ⓒ   3 days

    Ⓓ   4 days

13. The salesman sold $\frac{1}{3}$ of his inventory during a weekend sale. He had hoped to sell an even higher amount. Which fraction could represent the amount of his inventory he had hoped to sell?

    Ⓐ $\frac{1}{4}$

    Ⓑ $\frac{1}{8}$

    Ⓒ $\frac{1}{2}$

    Ⓓ $\frac{1}{6}$

14. One fifth of the tourists went to see the natural waterfall on Monday. Five fifths of them went to see it on Tuesday, and three fifth of them went to see it on Wednesday. List the days in ascending order according to the fraction of visitors who visited the waterfall.

Ⓐ Tuesday, Wednesday, Monday
Ⓑ Monday, Wednesday, Tuesday
Ⓒ Wednesday, Tuesday, Monday
Ⓓ Monday, Tuesday, Wednesday

15. What makes $\frac{4}{9} > \frac{4}{11}$?

Ⓐ The numerators are the same, so the first fraction is automatically greater.
Ⓑ Ninths are smaller than elevenths.
Ⓒ Ninths are larger than elevenths.
Ⓓ Ninths and elevenths are the same size.

16. Select the correct inequality sign that would go in between the fractions

		<	>	=
$\frac{24}{36}$	$\frac{2}{4}$	◯	◯	◯
$\frac{1}{4}$	$\frac{5}{11}$	◯	◯	◯
$\frac{10}{20}$	$\frac{7}{14}$	◯	◯	◯
$\frac{4}{4}$	$\frac{10}{11}$	◯	◯	◯

17. Circle all the fractions that are greater than $\frac{2}{3}$.

Ⓐ $\frac{30}{36}$

Ⓑ $\frac{3}{4}$

Ⓒ $\frac{5}{10}$

Ⓓ $\frac{30}{70}$

Ⓔ $\frac{9}{14}$

Ⓕ $\frac{7}{9}$

18. **Which of the following fractions make this statement true?**
    More than one answer maybe correct. Select all the correct answers
    $\frac{3}{5}$ > _____ .

Ⓐ $\frac{4}{5}$

Ⓑ $\frac{3}{10}$

Ⓒ $\frac{8}{15}$

Ⓓ $\frac{12}{20}$

Chapter 4

Lesson 3: Adding and Subtracting Fractions

You can scan the QR code given below or use the url to access additional EdSearch resources including videos and mobile apps related to *Adding and Subtracting Fractions.*

 **Adding and Subtracting Fractions**

URL	QR Code
http://www.lumoslearning.com/a/4nfb3a	

1. **Find the sum:**

   $\frac{3}{12} + \frac{2}{12} =$

   Ⓐ $\frac{5}{24}$

   Ⓑ $\frac{6}{12}$

   Ⓒ $\frac{5}{12}$

   Ⓓ $\frac{1}{4}$

2. **Find the sum:**

   $\frac{2}{7} + \frac{1}{7} =$

   Ⓐ $\frac{3}{7}$

   Ⓑ $\frac{3}{14}$

   Ⓒ $\frac{2}{14}$

   Ⓓ $\frac{1}{3}$

3. **What fraction expresses the total amount represented by the fraction models below?**

   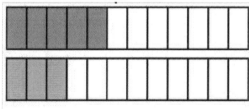

   =

   Ⓐ $\frac{1}{2}$

   Ⓑ $\frac{5}{12}$

   Ⓒ $\frac{2}{3}$

   Ⓓ $\frac{3}{4}$

4. **What fraction expresses the total amount represented by the fraction models?**

(A) $\frac{3}{5}$

(B) $\frac{3}{10}$

(C) $\frac{1}{2}$

(D) $\frac{3}{20}$

5. **Mary cut a pizza into 9 pieces. Mary ate 3 pieces, and Connie ate 3 pieces. What part of the pizza did they eat all together?**

(A) $\frac{9}{18}$

(B) $\frac{2}{3}$

(C) $\frac{6}{18}$

(D) $\frac{3}{4}$

6. Write the simplified fraction that will complete the equation.

$\frac{1}{4} + \frac{5}{10} =$

7. Select the correct fractions to complete each equation.

	$\frac{1}{2}$	$\frac{2}{5}$	$\frac{4}{9}$
$\frac{4}{5} - \frac{2}{5}$			
$\frac{1}{4} + \frac{4}{5}$			
$\frac{8}{9} - \frac{4}{9}$			

8. Write $2\frac{5}{8}$ as the sum of fractions. Select all the correct answers.

Ⓐ $2 + \frac{3}{8} + \frac{2}{8}$

Ⓑ $1 + \frac{4}{8} + \frac{1}{8}$

Ⓒ $1 + 1 + \frac{4}{8} + \frac{1}{8}$

Ⓓ $1 + \frac{2}{3} + \frac{3}{5}$

9. Find the difference. $7\frac{5}{9} - 5\frac{2}{9}$

Circle the correct answer.

Ⓐ $2\frac{4}{9}$

Ⓑ $2\frac{1}{9}$

Ⓒ $2\frac{5}{9}$

Ⓓ $2\frac{1}{3}$

Chapter 4

Lesson 4: Adding and Subtracting Fractions through Decompositions

You can scan the QR code given below or use the url to access additional EdSearch resources including videos and mobile apps related to *Adding and Subtracting Fractions through Decompositions*.

ed)Search *Adding and Subtracting Fractions through Decompositions*

URL	QR Code
http://www.lumoslearning.com/a/4nfb3b	

1. $1 \frac{1}{4} - \frac{3}{4} = \square$

   Ⓐ $\frac{6}{4} - \frac{3}{4} = \frac{3}{4}$

   Ⓑ $\frac{4}{4} - \frac{3}{4} = \frac{1}{4}$

   Ⓒ $\frac{4}{8} - \frac{3}{4} = \frac{1}{4}$

   Ⓓ $\frac{5}{4} - \frac{3}{4} = \frac{2}{4} = \frac{1}{2}$

2. How many sevenths are there in 3 whole pizza?

   Ⓐ 7
   Ⓑ 14
   Ⓒ 28
   Ⓓ 21

3. What fractional part could be added to each blank to make each number sentence true?

   $\frac{3}{8} = \frac{1}{8} + $ _____ $+$ _____ ;

   $\frac{3}{8} = $ _____ $+ \frac{2}{8}$

   Ⓐ $\frac{2}{8}$

   Ⓑ $\frac{1}{8}$

   Ⓒ $\frac{0}{8}$

   Ⓓ $\frac{3}{8}$

4. $2 \frac{3}{5} - \frac{4}{5} =$

   Ⓐ $1 \frac{1}{10}$

   Ⓑ $1 \frac{4}{5}$

   Ⓒ $1 \frac{2}{5}$

   Ⓓ $1 \frac{1}{5}$

5. How many sixths are there in 6 birthday cakes?

   Ⓐ 30
   Ⓑ 40
   Ⓒ 36
   Ⓓ 25

6 Match each fraction with its decomposition.

	$1\frac{2}{3}$	$2\frac{3}{5}$	$1\frac{1}{8}$
$1 + 1 + \frac{1}{5} + \frac{1}{5} + \frac{1}{5}$	○	○	○
$1 + \frac{1}{3} + \frac{1}{3}$	○	○	○
$1 + \frac{1}{8}$	○	○	○

7. What does the following add up to? $1+1+1+\frac{1}{8}+\frac{1}{8}+\frac{1}{8}$
   Write your answer in the box below.

8. $8\frac{3}{5} + \frac{4}{5}$. **Select all the correct answers.**

Ⓐ $8 + \frac{3}{5} + \frac{2}{5} + \frac{2}{5}$

Ⓑ $8 + \frac{7}{5}$

Ⓒ $8 + \frac{7}{10}$

Ⓓ $9 + \frac{2}{5}$

9. Solve $8\frac{1}{2} - 4\frac{3}{4}$.

   Circle the correct answer.

Ⓐ $4\frac{3}{4}$

Ⓑ $3\frac{3}{4}$

Ⓒ $3\frac{1}{4}$

Ⓓ $4\frac{1}{4}$

Chapter 4

Lesson 5: Adding and Subtracting Mixed Numbers

You can scan the QR code given below or use the url to access additional EdSearch resources including videos and mobile apps related to *Adding and Subtracting Mixed Numbers.*

 **Adding and Subtracting Mixed Numbers**

URL	QR Code
http://www.lumoslearning.com/a/4nfb3c	

1. Angelo picked 2 $\frac{3}{4}$ pounds of apples from the apple orchard. He gave 1 $\frac{1}{4}$ pounds to his neighbor Mrs. Mason. How many pounds of apples does Angelo have left?

   Ⓐ 1 $\frac{1}{2}$ pounds

   Ⓑ 1 $\frac{3}{4}$ pounds

   Ⓒ 2 $\frac{1}{4}$ pounds

   Ⓓ 1 $\frac{3}{8}$ pounds

2. Daniel and Colby are building a castle out of plastic building blocks. They will need 2 $\frac{1}{2}$ buckets of blocks for the castle. Daniel used to have two full buckets of blocks, but lost some, and now only has 1 $\frac{3}{4}$ buckets. Colby used to have two full buckets of blocks too, but now has 1 $\frac{1}{4}$ buckets. If Daniel and Colby combine their buckets of blocks, will they have enough to build their castle?

   Ⓐ No, they will have less than 1 $\frac{1}{2}$ buckets.

   Ⓑ No, they will have 1 $\frac{1}{2}$ buckets.

   Ⓒ Yes, they will have 2 $\frac{1}{2}$ buckets.

   Ⓓ Yes, they will have 3 buckets.

3. Lexi and Ava are making chocolate chip cookies for a sleepover with their friends. They will need 4 $\frac{1}{4}$ cups of chocolate chips to make enough cookies for their friends. Lexi has 2 $\frac{3}{4}$ cups of chocolate chips. Ava has 1 $\frac{3}{4}$ cups of chocolate chips. Will the girls have enough chocolate chips to make the cookies for their friends?

   Ⓐ They'll have less than 4 cups, but should just use the amount they have.

   Ⓑ They'll have less than 4 cups, so no.

   Ⓒ They'll have 4 $\frac{1}{4}$ cups, so yes.

   Ⓓ They'll have 4 $\frac{2}{4}$ cups, so yes.

4. 3 $\frac{2}{4}$ + 1 $\frac{1}{4}$ =

   Ⓐ $\frac{20}{4}$

   Ⓑ 2 $\frac{3}{4}$

   Ⓒ 4 $\frac{3}{4}$

   Ⓓ 5 $\frac{3}{4}$

5. $7\frac{9}{9} - 3\frac{5}{9} =$

Ⓐ $2\frac{7}{9}$

Ⓑ $3\frac{4}{9}$

Ⓒ $3\frac{3}{9}$

Ⓓ $4\frac{4}{9}$

6. What is $4\frac{2}{4} + 1\frac{2}{4}$?

[   ]

7. Match each equation with the correct answer.

	$2\frac{2}{4}$	$3\frac{3}{4}$	$4\frac{1}{4}$
$2\frac{1}{4} + 1\frac{2}{4}$	○	○	○
$5\frac{1}{4} - 2\frac{3}{4}$	○	○	○
$2\frac{3}{4} + 1\frac{2}{4}$	○	○	○

8. $6\frac{3}{8} + 5\frac{7}{8} = $? Circle all the correct answers.

Ⓐ $11\frac{10}{8}$

Ⓑ $11\frac{10}{16}$

Ⓒ $12\frac{1}{4}$

Ⓓ $\frac{49}{4}$

9. John picked $2\frac{2}{3}$ pounds of apples. Together, John and Jose picked $4\frac{1}{2}$ pounds of apples. How many pounds of apples did Jose pick? Highlight the correct answer.

Ⓐ $1\frac{5}{6}$

Ⓑ $1\frac{1}{6}$

Ⓒ $2\frac{5}{6}$

Ⓓ $2\frac{1}{6}$

Chapter 4

Lesson 6: Adding and Subtracting Fractions in Word Problems

You can scan the QR code given below or use the url to access additional EdSearch resources including videos and mobile apps related to *Adding and Subtracting Fractions in Word Problems*.

 **Adding and Subtracting Fractions in Word Problems**

URL	QR Code
http://www.lumoslearning.com/a/4nfb3d	

1. Marcie and Lisa wanted to share a cheese pizza. Marcie ate $\frac{3}{6}$ of the pizza, and Lisa ate $\frac{2}{6}$ of the pizza. How much of the pizza did the girls eat together?

   Ⓐ $\frac{6}{6}$ of a pizza

   Ⓑ $\frac{5}{6}$ of a pizza

   Ⓒ $\frac{1}{2}$ of a pizza

   Ⓓ $\frac{4}{6}$ of a pizza

2. Sophie and Angie need $8\frac{5}{8}$ feet of ribbon to package gift baskets. Sophie has $3\frac{1}{8}$ feet of ribbon and Angie has $5\frac{3}{8}$ feet of ribbon. Will the girls have enough ribbon to complete the gift baskets?

   Ⓐ Yes, and they will have extra ribbon.
   Ⓑ Yes, but they will not have extra ribbon.
   Ⓒ They will have just enough ribbon to make the baskets.
   Ⓓ No, they will not have enough ribbon to make the baskets.

3. Travis has $4\frac{1}{8}$ pizzas left over from his soccer party. After giving some pizza to his friend, he has $2\frac{4}{8}$ of a pizza left. How much pizza did Travis give to his friend?

   Ⓐ $1\frac{1}{2}$ pizzas

   Ⓑ $1\frac{5}{8}$ pizzas

   Ⓒ $1\frac{3}{4}$ pizzas

   Ⓓ $1\frac{5}{7}$ pizzas

4. **Which student solved the problem correctly?**

Student 1	Student 2	Student 3
$3 + 2 = 5$ and $\frac{3}{4} + \frac{1}{4} = 1$ so $5 + 1 = 6$	$3\frac{3}{4} + 2 = 5\frac{3}{4}$ and $5\frac{3}{4} + \frac{1}{4} = 5\frac{4}{4} = 6$	$3\frac{3}{4} = \frac{15}{4}$ and $2\frac{1}{4} = \frac{9}{4}$ so $\frac{15}{4} + \frac{9}{4} = \frac{24}{4} = 6$

Ⓐ Student 1
Ⓑ Student 2
Ⓒ Student 3
Ⓓ All of the students

5. **There are 2 loaves of freshly baked bread, and each loaf is cut into 8 equal pieces. If $\frac{5}{8}$ of a loaf is used for breakfast, and $\frac{7}{8}$ of a loaf is used for lunch, what fraction of the bread if left?**

Ⓐ $\frac{1}{2}$

Ⓑ $\frac{1}{16}$

Ⓒ $\frac{1}{8}$

Ⓓ $\frac{1}{10}$

6. **Tom and Sally buy a box of chocolates. Tom eats $\frac{2}{7}$ of the chocolates. Sally eats $\frac{3}{7}$ of the chocolates. What fraction of chocolates did they eat altogether? Write your answer in the box given below**

7. Match each of the word problem with the correct answer

	$\frac{3}{5}$	$\frac{2}{3}$
There are two bags of candy. The first bag has $\frac{2}{5}$ of a bag, and the second has $\frac{1}{5}$ of a bag. What fraction of a bag of candy is there in all?	◯	◯
Izabel has a bag of marbles, but lets her brother have $\frac{1}{3}$ of them. What fraction represents how much she has left?	◯	◯

8 John and his friends ate $3\frac{1}{3}$ pizzas on Monday. They ate $2\frac{1}{4}$ pizzas on Tuesday. How much of the pizza did they eat in all? Select all the correct answers.

Ⓐ $5\frac{7}{12}$ pizzas

Ⓑ $5\frac{2}{7}$ pizzas

Ⓒ $\frac{37}{7}$ pizzas

Ⓓ $\frac{67}{12}$ pizzas

9. Jose had $5\frac{5}{12}$ m of ribbon. He used $3\frac{7}{8}$ m of the ribbon. How much ribbon did he have left? Mark the correct answer.

Ⓐ $2\frac{13}{24}$ m

Ⓑ $1\frac{3}{24}$ m

Ⓒ $1\frac{13}{24}$ m

Ⓓ $1\frac{9}{24}$ m

Chapter 4

Lesson 7: Multiplying Fractions

You can scan the QR code given below or use the url to access additional EdSearch resources including videos and mobile apps related to *Multiplying Fractions*.

URL	QR Code
http://www.lumoslearning.com/a/4nfb4a	

ed Search **Multiplying Fractions**

1. Solve $\frac{1}{2}$ x 6 =

    Ⓐ $\frac{2}{6}$

    Ⓑ $\frac{1}{3}$

    Ⓒ 3

    Ⓓ $\frac{3}{6}$

2. Solve 6 x $\frac{1}{4}$ =

    Ⓐ 2

    Ⓑ $1\frac{1}{2}$

    Ⓒ $\frac{4}{6}$

    Ⓓ 3

3. What product do these models show?

    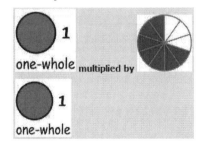

    Ⓐ $\frac{4}{10}$

    Ⓑ $\frac{14}{100}$

    Ⓒ $\frac{7}{10}$

    Ⓓ $1\frac{4}{10}$

4. Find the product:
    45 x $\frac{2}{3}$

    Ⓐ 90

    Ⓑ 86

    Ⓒ 30

    Ⓓ 129

5. Select all of the multiplication problems that will give us $\frac{1}{2}$ as our simplified answer.

Ⓐ $\frac{2}{3}$ x $\frac{2}{3}$

Ⓑ $\frac{2}{3}$ x $\frac{3}{4}$

Ⓒ $\frac{1}{2}$ x $\frac{10}{11}$

Ⓓ $\frac{3}{5}$ x $\frac{5}{6}$

Ⓔ $\frac{1}{4}$ x $\frac{2}{6}$

6. Write the fraction that will make the equation true. $\frac{1}{3}$ x $\frac{8}{10}$ Write your answer in the box given below

7. Match each equation with its answer

	$\frac{8}{25}$	$\frac{1}{25}$	$\frac{1}{16}$
$\frac{4}{5}$ x $\frac{2}{5}$	◯	◯	◯
$\frac{1}{4}$ x $\frac{1}{4}$	◯	◯	◯
$\frac{2}{5}$ x $\frac{4}{10}$	◯	◯	◯

8. Which of the following are equal to 5 x $\frac{2}{7}$. Select all the correct answers.

Ⓐ $\frac{10}{7}$

Ⓑ $\frac{2}{14}$

Ⓒ $1\frac{3}{7}$

Ⓓ $\frac{2}{7}$ + $\frac{2}{7}$ + $\frac{2}{7}$ + $\frac{2}{7}$ + $\frac{2}{7}$

Chapter 4

Lesson 8: Multiplying Fractions by a Whole Number

You can scan the QR code given below or use the url to access additional EdSearch resources including videos and mobile apps related to *Multiplying Fractions by a Whole Number.*

 Multiplying Fractions by a Whole Number

URL	QR Code
http://www.lumoslearning.com/a/4nfb4b	

1. **7 x $\frac{1}{3}$ =**

    Ⓐ $\frac{1}{21}$

    Ⓑ $\frac{3}{7}$

    Ⓒ $\frac{7}{22}$

    Ⓓ $\frac{7}{3}$

2. Cook is making sandwiches for the party. If each person at a party eats $\frac{2}{8}$ of a pound of turkey, and there are 5 people at the party, how many pounds of turkey are needed?

    Ⓐ 3 pounds

    Ⓑ 1$\frac{1}{4}$ pounds

    Ⓒ 2$\frac{1}{4}$ pounds

    Ⓓ $\frac{4}{8}$ pounds

3. $\frac{1}{5}$ **x 7 =**

    Ⓐ $\frac{7}{5}$

    Ⓑ $\frac{5}{7}$

    Ⓒ 35

    Ⓓ $\frac{1}{7}$

4. $\frac{1}{9}$ **x 8 =**

    Ⓐ 72

    Ⓑ $\frac{8}{9}$

    Ⓒ $\frac{1}{8}$

    Ⓓ $\frac{9}{8}$

5. **Which product is greater than 1?**

    Ⓐ $2 \times \dfrac{2}{3}$

    Ⓑ $4 \times \dfrac{1}{6}$

    Ⓒ $3 \times \dfrac{2}{10}$

    Ⓓ $2 \times \dfrac{2}{5}$

6. **Fill in the missing number to complete the equation.** $\dfrac{1}{2} \times \underline{\quad} = 4$

7. **Match the problem with the correct answer**

	$2\dfrac{2}{3}$	2	3
$\left(\dfrac{1}{3}\right) \times 6$	○	○	○
$\left(\dfrac{2}{3}\right) \times 4$	○	○	○
$\left(\dfrac{3}{4}\right) \times 4$	○	○	○

8. **Which of the following are equal to $3 \times \dfrac{7}{6}$. Select all the correct answers.**

    Ⓐ $\dfrac{21}{6}$

    Ⓑ $\dfrac{10}{6}$

    Ⓒ $3\dfrac{1}{2}$

    Ⓓ $\dfrac{7}{6} + \dfrac{7}{6} + \dfrac{7}{6}$

Chapter 4

Lesson 9: Multiplying Fractions in Word Problems

You can scan the QR code given below or use the url to access additional EdSearch resources including videos and mobile apps related to *FMultiplying Fractions in Word Problems*.

 Multiplying Fractions in Word Problems

URL	QR Code
http://www.lumoslearning.com/a/4nfb4c	

1. Aimee is making treat bags for her Christmas party. She is going to put $\frac{2}{3}$ cups of mint M&Ms in each bag. She has invited 9 friends to her party. How many cups of mint M&Ms does she need for her friends' treat bags?

Ⓐ 5 cups
Ⓑ 6 cups
Ⓒ 4 cups
Ⓓ 5 $\frac{1}{2}$ cups

2. Aimee was making treat bags from Question #1, but then she decided to also include $\frac{1}{2}$ of a cup of coconut M&Ms in each bag. How many cups of coconut M&Ms does she need? (Remember that she has 9 friends.)

Ⓐ 4 $\frac{1}{2}$ cups
Ⓑ 4 cups
Ⓒ 3 $\frac{1}{3}$ cups
Ⓓ 3 cups

3. Aimee's mom bought palm tree bags to celebrate their move to Florida. This is their first Christmas in Florida. Each treat bag will hold one cup of treats. Aimee wants to use $\frac{2}{3}$ cup mint M&M's and $\frac{1}{2}$ cup coconut M&M's. Will Aimee be able to fit all of the M&Ms in each party bag for her friends?

Ⓐ Yes
Ⓑ No

4. Kendra runs $\frac{3}{4}$ mile each day. How many miles does she run in 1 week?

Ⓐ 5 miles
Ⓑ 5 $\frac{1}{4}$ miles
Ⓒ 5 $\frac{1}{2}$ miles
Ⓓ 5 $\frac{3}{4}$ miles

5. Mrs. Howett is making a punch. The punch uses $\frac{3}{5}$ cup of grapefruit juice for one serving. If she makes 4 servings, how many cups of grapefruit juice does she need?

Ⓐ 2 $\frac{2}{5}$ cups
Ⓑ 1 $\frac{2}{5}$ cups
Ⓒ 3 $\frac{1}{5}$ cups
Ⓓ 1 $\frac{4}{5}$ cups

6. Tim has 3 cups of milk. He used 1/3 of the milk. How many cups of milk are left?

7. Match each of the problem with the correct answer choice.

	$40	$60
The dinner for a large family costs $80. Mr. Smith has a $\frac{1}{2}$ off coupon, so what will the final price be?	○	○
The movie tickets cost $90 but I have a coupon for $\frac{1}{3}$ off. How much will I spend?	○	○

8. John can paint $\frac{2}{5}$ of a table in 15 minutes. Jose can paint 8 times that amount in 15 minutes. How many tables can Jose paint in 15 minutes? Circle the correct answer.

Ⓐ $2\frac{3}{5}$

Ⓑ $\frac{1}{20}$

Ⓒ $3\frac{2}{5}$

Ⓓ $3\frac{1}{5}$

Chapter 4

Lesson 10: 10 to 100 Equivalent Fractions

You can scan the QR code given below or use the url to access additional EdSearch resources including videos and mobile apps related to *10 to 100 Equivalent Fractions*.

 10 to 100 Equivalent Fractions

URL	QR Code
http://www.lumoslearning.com/a/4nfc5	

1. **What fraction of a dollar is 6 dimes and 3 pennies?**

   Ⓐ 0.63 or $\frac{63}{100}$

   Ⓑ 0.73 or $\frac{73}{100}$

   Ⓒ 0.53 or $\frac{53}{100}$

   Ⓓ 0.43 or $\frac{43}{100}$

2. **1 tenth + 4 hundredths = _____ hundredths**

   Ⓐ 14
   Ⓑ 140
   Ⓒ 1400
   Ⓓ 104

3. **5 tenths + 2 hundredths = _____ hundredths**

   Ⓐ 25
   Ⓑ 525
   Ⓒ 52
   Ⓓ 502

4. **5 hundredths + 2 tenths = _____ hundredths**

   Ⓐ 25
   Ⓑ 52
   Ⓒ 252
   Ⓓ 502

5. **14 hundredths = _____ hundredths + 4 hundredths**

   Ⓐ 144
   Ⓑ 414
   Ⓒ 104
   Ⓓ 10

LumosLearning.com

6. 14 hundredths = _____ tenths + 4 hundredths

    Ⓐ 10
    Ⓑ 100
    Ⓒ 1
    Ⓓ 0

7. 14 hundredths = 1 tenth + 3 hundredths + _____ hundredths

    Ⓐ 10
    Ⓑ 1
    Ⓒ 0
    Ⓓ 4

8. 80 hundredths = _____ tenths

    Ⓐ 8
    Ⓑ 80
    Ⓒ 0
    Ⓓ 1

9. $\frac{2}{10} + \frac{41}{100} =$

    Ⓐ $\frac{43}{100}$

    Ⓑ $\frac{43}{10}$

    Ⓒ $\frac{61}{100}$

    Ⓓ $\frac{61}{10}$

10. Match each fraction to its equivalent.

	$\frac{10}{100}$	$\frac{60}{100}$	$\frac{90}{100}$
$\frac{9}{10}$	○	○	○
$\frac{1}{10}$	○	○	○
$\frac{6}{10}$	○	○	○

11. Select the equivalent fraction of $\frac{2}{10}$ that has a denominator of 100. Circle the correct answer.

Ⓐ $\frac{12}{100}$

Ⓑ $\frac{12}{100}$

Ⓒ $\frac{20}{100}$

Ⓓ $\frac{1}{5}$

12. Write the equivalent fraction of $\frac{4}{10}$ that now has a denominator of 100. Instruction: Write in the format $\frac{A}{B}$.

13. Solve $8\frac{5}{100}$ - 5

Ⓐ $2\frac{75}{100}$

Ⓑ $3\frac{75}{100}$

Ⓒ $2\frac{3}{4}$

Ⓓ $3\frac{3}{4}$

Chapter 4

Lesson 11: Convert Fractions to Decimals

You can scan the QR code given below or use the url to access additional EdSearch resources including videos and mobile apps related to *Convert Fractions to Decimals*.

 **Convert Fractions to Decimals**

URL	QR Code
http://www.lumoslearning.com/a/4nfc6	

1. Point A is located closest to _____ on this number line?

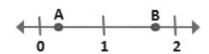

Ⓐ 0
Ⓑ 0.75
Ⓒ 0.25
Ⓓ -1

2. Convert $\frac{148}{1000}$ to a decimal.

Ⓐ 0.148
Ⓑ 14.8
Ⓒ .00148
Ⓓ 0.0148

3. Where is Point D located on this number line?

Ⓐ -2.5
Ⓑ -2
Ⓒ -1.5
Ⓓ -3

4. Convert 129 $\frac{1}{4}$ to decimal.

Ⓐ 129.25
Ⓑ 129.025
Ⓒ 129.75
Ⓓ 129.14

5. Convert the fraction to a decimal: $\frac{3}{1000}$ = _____

Ⓐ 0.03
Ⓑ 0.003
Ⓒ 0.30
Ⓓ 0.0003

6. **What decimal does this model represent?**

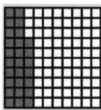

Ⓐ 2.7
Ⓑ 2.0
Ⓒ 0.207
Ⓓ 0.27

7. **Mr. Hughes preferred to convert this decimal into a fraction in order to add it to a group of other fractions. Which answer is correct?**
   0.044

   Ⓐ $\frac{44}{100}$

   Ⓑ $\frac{44}{10000}$

   Ⓒ $\frac{44}{1000}$

   Ⓓ $\frac{44}{10}$

8. **Convert the mixed number to a decimal:** $1\frac{4}{1000}$ = _____

   Ⓐ 1.04
   Ⓑ 1.004
   Ⓒ 1.4
   Ⓓ .1004

9. **The construction crew was working 0.193 of the times that we traveled that road. What fraction of the time was the crew working?**

   Ⓐ $\frac{193}{100}$

   Ⓑ $\frac{193}{10000}$

   Ⓒ $\frac{193}{1000}$

   Ⓓ $\frac{193}{10}$

10. What are the addends in this problem?
    0.300 + 0.249

Ⓐ $\frac{300}{100} + \frac{249}{100}$

Ⓑ $\frac{300}{100} + \frac{249}{1000}$

Ⓒ $\frac{549}{1000}$

Ⓓ $\frac{300}{1000} + \frac{249}{1000}$

11. Match each fraction to its decimal.

	0.50	0.25	0.10
$\frac{1}{2}$	○	○	○
$\frac{1}{4}$	○	○	○
$\frac{1}{10}$	○	○	○

12. Circle all the fractions that are equivalent to 0.25.

Ⓐ $\frac{1}{2}$

Ⓑ $\frac{1}{4}$

Ⓒ $\frac{9}{10}$

Ⓓ $\frac{3}{5}$

Ⓔ $\frac{25}{100}$

13. Write the decimal that is equivalent to $\frac{1}{20}$. Write your answer in the box below.

14. Which of the following numbers are equal to $\frac{6}{10}$? Select all the correct answers.

Ⓐ 0.6

Ⓑ 0.06

Ⓒ $\frac{60}{100}$

Ⓓ 0.60

Chapter 4

Lesson 12: Compare Decimals

You can scan the QR code given below or use the url to access additional EdSearch resources including videos and mobile apps related to *Compare Decimals*.

ed)Search	**Compare Decimals**
URL	**QR Code**
http://www.lumoslearning.com/a/4nfc7	

1. **Point B is located closest to ____ on this number line.**

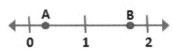

Ⓐ 1.75
Ⓑ 1.5
Ⓒ 2.25
Ⓓ 1.1

2. **Compare the following decimals using <, >, or =.**
   0.05 ___ 0.50

   Ⓐ 0.05 < 0.50
   Ⓑ 0.05 = 0.50
   Ⓒ 0.05 > 0.50

3. **The rainbow trout dinner costs $23.99. The steak dinner costs $26.49. The roast chicken dinner is $5.00 less than $30.79. Which dinner costs the most?**

   Ⓐ rainbow trout dinner
   Ⓑ steak dinner
   Ⓒ chicken dinner

4. **Compare the following decimals using <, >, or =.**
   0.2 ___ 0.200

   Ⓐ 0.2 < 0.200
   Ⓑ 0.2 = 0.200
   Ⓒ 0.2 > 0.200

5. **Which of these decimals is the greatest?**
   0.0060
   0.006
   0.060

   Ⓐ 0.0060
   Ⓑ 0.006
   Ⓒ 0.060

6. **Which comparison symbol makes this statement true?**
   1.954 ___ 0.1954

   Ⓐ 1.954 = 0.1954
   Ⓑ 1.954 > 0.1954
   Ⓒ 1.954 < 0.1954

7. Order these decimals from least to greatest.
   43.75; 0.4385; 0.04375

   (A) 0.04375; 43.75; 0.4385
   (B) 0.4385; 0.04375; 43.75
   (C) 0.04375; 0.4385; 43.75
   (D) 0.4385; 43.75; 0.04375

8. Compare the following decimals using <, >, or =.
   1.10 ____ 1.1000

   (A) 1.10 < 1.1000
   (B) 1.10 = 1.1000
   (C) 1.10 > 1.1000

9. A one-way airline ticket to Atlanta from New York costs $65.00 more on the weekend than it does during the week. How much would a $225 (weekday price) ticket cost if the traveler needed to fly on a Saturday?

   (A) $270.00
   (B) $290.00
   (C) $280.00
   (D) $300.00

10. A pattern exists in the prices of the following vehicles. Which numbers complete this table?

Vehicle	Price
compact car	$30,000.00
midsize car	$35,000.00
luxury car	$40,000.00
jeep	?
mini van	$50,000.00
full size van	?

   (A) $36,000.00; $51,000.00
   (B) $45,000.00; $55,000.00
   (C) $40,000.00; $51,000.00
   (D) $36,000.00; $55,000.00

11. Observe the decimals numbers given below. 0.93, 0.39, 0.84, 0.09
    Which number is the largest ? Identify the number and write it in the box given below

```
┌─────────────────────────────┐
│                             │
│                             │
│                             │
└─────────────────────────────┘
```

12. Match the number pair with the correct inequality sign.

	<	>	=
0.25 _ 0.39	○	○	○
0.89 _ 0.890	○	○	○
0.12 _ 0.21	○	○	○
0.29 _ 0.28	○	○	○

13. Circle all the decimals that are less than 0.45.

    0.28, 0.96, 0.39, 0.42 , 0.58, 0.04, 0.37, 0.49

14. Two decimal numbers X and Y are represented by the two area models below. Compare
    the two numbers. From among the 4 options given below, identify the correct statement
    and write it in the box given below.

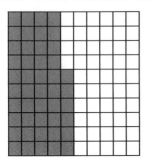 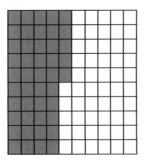

    x > y
    x = y
    x < y

```
┌─────────────────────────────┐
│                             │
│                             │
│                             │
└─────────────────────────────┘
```

15. Compare the first number with the second number in each row and fill the table by writing the correct inequality sign in the table.

First Number	Symbol	Second Number
8 ones and 5 hundredths	<	8.5
$7\frac{56}{10}$		7.56
5 tenths		25 hundredths
6.52		65 tenths and 2 hundredths

End of Number & Operations - Fractions

Chapter 5:
Measurement and Data

Lesson 1: Units of Measurement

You can scan the QR code given below or use the url to access additional EdSearch resources including videos and mobile apps related to *Units of Measurement*.

Categories   About 4 results (0.007 seconds)

- Khan Academy (2)
- Videos (2)
- Popular Searches ▼
- Recent Searches ▼

Unit sense

Resource: Videos
The truth is that you can use almost any unit of measurement as long as you're willing for that number to be really big or really small. The key is to find the most reasonable unit. Can you help?...

REASONABLE UNIT OF MEASUREMENT

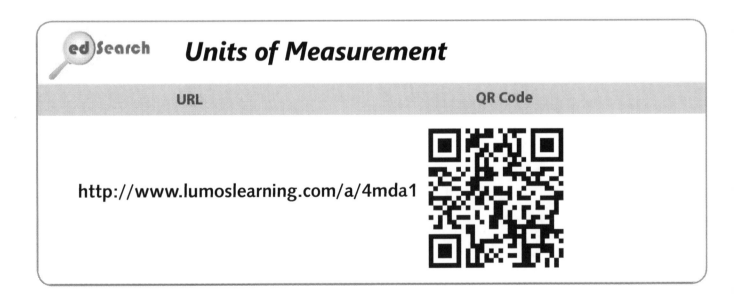

ed Search   **Units of Measurement**

URL	QR Code
http://www.lumoslearning.com/a/4mda1	

1. **What customary unit should be used to measure the weight of the table shown in the picture below?**

Ⓐ pounds
Ⓑ inches
Ⓒ kilograms
Ⓓ tons

2. **Which of the following is an appropriate customary unit to measure the weight of a small bird?**

Ⓐ grams
Ⓑ ounces
Ⓒ pounds
Ⓓ units

3. **Complete the following statement:**
   A horse might weigh _____.

Ⓐ about 500 pounds
Ⓑ about 12 pounds
Ⓒ about a gallon
Ⓓ about 200 ounces

4. **Choose the appropriate customary unit to measure the length of a road.**

Ⓐ Yard
Ⓑ Meter
Ⓒ Kilometer
Ⓓ Mile

5. **Choose the appropriate unit to measure the height of a tall tree.**

Ⓐ miles
Ⓑ yards
Ⓒ centimeters
Ⓓ gallons

6. **Which of the following is not a customary unit?**

   Ⓐ Kilograms
   Ⓑ Yards
   Ⓒ Pounds
   Ⓓ Miles

7. **Which of the following is a customary unit that can be used to measure the volume of a liquid?**

   Ⓐ yards
   Ⓑ fluid ounces
   Ⓒ milliliters
   Ⓓ pounds

8. **Which is more, 18 teaspoons or 2 fluid ounces?**

   Ⓐ 2 fluid ounces
   Ⓑ They are equal.
   Ⓒ 18 teaspoons

9. **A math textbook might weigh _____ .**

   Ⓐ 125 ounces
   Ⓑ 25 ounces
   Ⓒ 200 ounces
   Ⓓ 2 ounces

10. **To make the medicine seem to taste better, Mom told Bonita she had to take tablespoons instead of teaspoons. How many tablespoons of medicine should Bonita take if the dose is 3 teaspoons?**

    Ⓐ tablespoons
    Ⓑ 1 tablespoon
    Ⓒ 6 tablespoons
    Ⓓ 1/2 tablespoon

11. How many kilometers are there in 4,000 meters? Write your answer in the box below

```
(                    )
```

12. Match each row with the correct conversion

	4	5	6
360 min = ___ hr	○	○	○
500 cm = ___ m	○	○	○
240 sec = ___ min	○	○	○

13. Fill in the table with the conversion as indicated in the header column

km	m	cm
6.5	6,500	650,000
8.2		
	7,300	
		825,000

14. Complete the following. 44 pints = ? and select all the correct answers.

Ⓐ 88 cups
Ⓑ 22 cups
Ⓒ 88 quarts
Ⓓ 22 quarts
Ⓔ 5.5 gallons
Ⓕ 11 gallons

Chapter 5

Lesson 2: Measurement Problems

You can scan the QR code given below or use the url to access additional EdSearch resources including videos and mobile apps related to *Measurement Problems*.

 **Search**   ***Measurement Problems***

URL	QR Code
http://www.lumoslearning.com/a/4mda2	

1. Arthur wants to arrive at soccer practice at 5:30 PM. He knows it takes him 42 minutes to walk to practice from his house. Estimate the time Arthur should leave his house to go to practice?

   Ⓐ 5:00 PM
   Ⓑ 4:45 PM
   Ⓒ 4:30 PM
   Ⓓ 3:45 PM

2. A baseball game began at 7:05 PM and lasted for 2 hours and 38 minutes. At what time did the game end?

   Ⓐ 9:43 PM
   Ⓑ 10:33 PM
   Ⓒ 9:38 PM
   Ⓓ 9:33 PM

3. 4 feet and 5 inches is the same as:

   Ⓐ 48 inches
   Ⓑ 53 inches
   Ⓒ 41 inches
   Ⓓ 65 inches

4. Amir bought two cowboy hats for $47, a pair of cowboy boots for $150, and a leather belt for $32. The tax was $13.74. He gave the cashier $300. How much change does she owe him?

   Ⓐ $242.74
   Ⓑ $13.74
   Ⓒ $57.26
   Ⓓ $257.26

5. Harriet needed $\frac{1}{2}$ cup of milk for the white sauce, but she could only find her tablespoon to measure with. How many tablespoons of milk will she need?

   Ⓐ 4 tablespoons
   Ⓑ 6 tablespoons
   Ⓒ 8 tablespoons
   Ⓓ 10 tablespoons

6. Use a comparison symbol to complete the following statement:
   32 ounces ___ 1 pound

   Ⓐ <
   Ⓑ =
   Ⓒ >

7. Rachel's gymnastics lessons lasted for 1 year. Sharon's lessons lasted for 9 months. Yolanda's lessons lasted for 23 months. How much time did the girls spend on lessons altogether?

   Ⓐ 4 years, 0 months
   Ⓑ 3 years, 0 months
   Ⓒ 3 years, 8 months
   Ⓓ 4 years, 8 months

8. To make some of the best cookies, mix 1 cup of butter, 2 cups of sugar, $2\frac{1}{2}$ cups of flour, $2\frac{1}{2}$ teaspoons of vanilla extract, $\frac{1}{2}$ teaspoon of baking soda, and $\frac{3}{4}$ cups of chocolate chips. Which comparison symbols would complete the following statements?

   amount of flour ___ amount of butter
   amount of butter ___ amount of sugar

   Ⓐ >; =
   Ⓑ <; >
   Ⓒ >; <
   Ⓓ <; =

9. The bookstore is selling paperback books for $3.25 each. How much would 4 paperback books cost?

   Ⓐ $12.00
   Ⓑ $13.00
   Ⓒ $13.50
   Ⓓ $12.50

10. If Cindy bought 3 DVDs and 2 nacho kits, how much would she pay for all items before taxes? Use the table below to answer the question:

Item	Unit Price
CDs	$10.99
DVDs	$24.99
Cordless Phone	$30.00
Flash Drives	$9.99
Nacho Kits	$6.99

Ⓐ $31.98
Ⓑ $74.97
Ⓒ $84.95
Ⓓ $88.95

11. Sam was measuring out 6 cups of milk, but his measuring cup only measured 2 cups. How many times does he fill the measuring cup? Write your answer in the box below

12. Select the correct answer for each row.

	$2\frac{1}{4}$	$4\frac{1}{4}$
I need 5 cups of flour for my recipe. I need ¾ cup more. How much flour did I start with?	○	○
I want to make a tug of war rope. It has to be 16 feet long. I have 18 feet 9 inches of rope. How much will I have to cut off? Express your answer as a mixed number in feet.	○	○

13. Complete the table.

On Thursday, the restaurant used 2 cups less sugar than they used on Friday. On Friday, they used 22 cups. On Saturday, they used 3 more than on Friday. What was the total amount of sugar used over those three days?	
Anna was cutting wood. She cut 5 cords of wood on Monday, 1 less than that on Tuesday, and 3 more than that on Wednesday (compared to Monday). How much wood did she cut in all?	

14. Greg rode his bicycle some distance in the past 5 days. He covers $2\frac{1}{4}$ km every day. How much distance did he cover in 5 days? Express your answer

   Ⓐ 1,125 meters
   Ⓑ 12,250 meters
   Ⓒ 1,125 meters
   Ⓓ 11,250 meters

Chapter 5

Lesson 3: Perimeter & Area

You can scan the QR code given below or use the url to access additional EdSearch resources including videos and mobile apps related to *Perimeter & Area.*

 **Perimeter & Area**

URL	QR Code
http://www.lumoslearning.com/a/4mda3	

1. **A rectangular room measures 10 feet long and 13 feet wide. How could you find out the area of this room?**

    Ⓐ Add 10 and 13, then double the results
    Ⓑ Multiply 10 by 13
    Ⓒ Add 10 and 13
    Ⓓ None of the above

2. **A rectangle has a perimeter of 30 inches. Which of the following could be the dimensions of the rectangle?**

    Ⓐ 10 inches long and 5 inches wide
    Ⓑ 6 inches long and 5 inches wide
    Ⓒ 10 inches long and 3 inches wide
    Ⓓ 15 inches long and 15 inches wide

    48 feet

    Figure A

    36 feet

3. **Which of these expressions could be used to find the perimeter of the above figure?**

    Ⓐ 48 + 36 + 2
    Ⓑ 48 x 36
    Ⓒ 2 x (48 + 36)
    Ⓓ 48 + 36

4. **A chalkboard is 72 inches long and 30 inches wide. What is its perimeter?**

    Ⓐ 204 inches
    Ⓑ 2,160 inches
    Ⓒ 102 inches
    Ⓓ 2,100 inches

5. **Which of the following statements is true?**

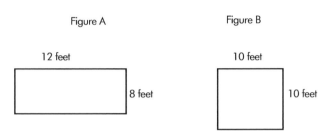

Figure A   Figure B

12 feet   10 feet

8 feet   10 feet

Ⓐ The two shapes have the same perimeter.
Ⓑ The two shapes have the same area.
Ⓒ The two figures are congruent.
Ⓓ Figure A has a greater area than Figure B.

6. **If a square has a perimeter of 100 units, how long is each of its sides?**

Ⓐ 10 units
Ⓑ 20 units
Ⓒ 25 units
Ⓓ Not enough information is given.

7. **Find the perimeter of Shape C.**

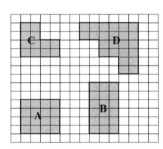

□ = 1 square unit

Ⓐ 8 units
Ⓑ 12 units
Ⓒ 14 units
Ⓓ 16 units

8. **Find the area of Shape C.**

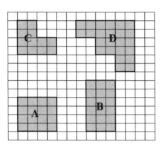

$\square$ = 1 square unit

Ⓐ 8 square units
Ⓑ 12 square units
Ⓒ 14 square units
Ⓓ 16 square units

9. **What is the perimeter of this shape?**

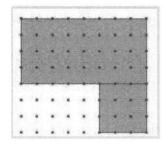

Ⓐ 24 units
Ⓑ 28 units
Ⓒ 30 units
Ⓓ 34 units

10. **A rectangle has an area of 48 square units and a perimeter of 32 units. What are its dimensions?**

Ⓐ 6 units by 8 units
Ⓑ 12 units by 4 units
Ⓒ 16 units by 3 units
Ⓓ All of the above are possible.

11. **What is the perimeter of the following 6 cm by 4 cm rectangle? Write the answer in the box given below**

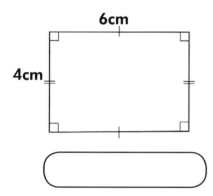

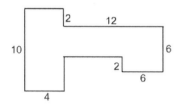

12. **Match perimeter and area to its correct value for the figure shown**

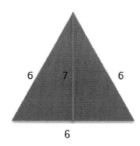

	100	56	102
Perimeter: ___ units			
Area: ___ units squared	◯	◯	◯

13. **Fill in the correct perimeter and area for the following shape.**

Area	
Perimeter	

14. **If the area of a square paper is 144 sq. feet, what is the length of any side of the paper? Circle the correct answer.**

12 feet, 36 feet, 18 feet, 6 feet

Ⓐ 12 feet
Ⓑ 36 feet
Ⓒ 18 feet
Ⓓ 6 feet

Chapter 5

Lesson 4: Representing and Interpreting Data

You can scan the QR code given below or use the url to access additional EdSearch resources including videos and mobile apps related to *Representing and Interpreting Data*.

 Representing and Interpreting Data

URL	QR Code
http://www.lumoslearning.com/a/4mdb4	

1. **The students in Mrs. Riley's class were asked how many cousins they have. The results are shown in the line plot. Use the information shown in the line plot to respond to the following.**
   How many of the students have no cousins?

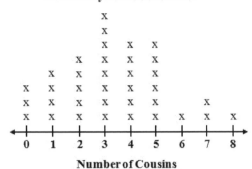

Ⓐ 0 students
Ⓑ 1 student
Ⓒ 2 students
Ⓓ 3 students

2. **The students in Mrs. Riley's class were asked how many cousins they have. The results are shown in the line plot. Use the information shown in the line plot to respond to the following.**
   How many of the students have exactly 4 cousins?

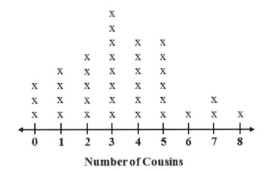

Ⓐ 1 student
Ⓑ 5 students
Ⓒ 6 students
Ⓓ 7 students

3. According to this graph, which are the 2 most favorite foods people enjoy at a carnival?

Favorite Carnival Foods

caramel apples	elephant ears	corn dogs	cotton candy	french fries	candy apples	funnel cakes
x			x			
x			x		x	x
x			x		x	x
x			x		x	x
x		x	x		x	x
x		x	x		x	x
x	x	x	x		x	x
x	x	x	x		x	x
x	x	x	x	x	x	x
x	x	x	x	x	x	x
x	x	x	x	x	x	x

Ⓐ candy apples and funnel cake
Ⓑ caramel apples and cotton candy
Ⓒ cotton candy and funnel cake
Ⓓ caramel apples and candy apples

4. How many more families prepare the night before the picnic than prepare right before leaving for the picnic?

Families That Pack the Night Before the Picnic	Families That Rise Early in the Morning to Pack for the Picnic	Families That Pack Right Before They Leave for the Picnic
x		
x	x	
x	x	x
x	x	x

(Each X is worth 2 points.)

Ⓐ 2
Ⓑ 4
Ⓒ 1
Ⓓ 8

5. **The school nurse kept track of how many students visited her clinic during a week. She plotted the results on a line graph. Use the line graph to respond to the following. What trend should the nurse notice?**

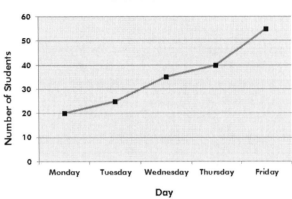

Ⓐ The number of students visiting her office increased throughout the week.
Ⓑ The number of students visiting her office decreased throughout the week.
Ⓒ The number of students visiting her office remained constant throughout the week.
Ⓓ There is no apparent trend.

6. **The school nurse kept track of how many students visited her clinic during a week. She plotted the results on a line graph. Use the line graph to respond to the following. How many more students visited the nurse on Friday than on Monday?**

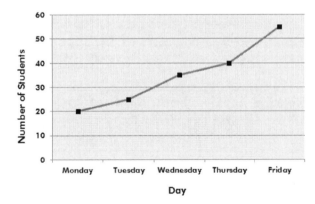

Ⓐ 20 students
Ⓑ 35 students
Ⓒ 45 students
Ⓓ 55 students

7. The school nurse kept track of how many students visited her office during a week. She plotted the results on a line graph. Use the line graph to respond to the following. How many students visited the nurse on Wednesday?

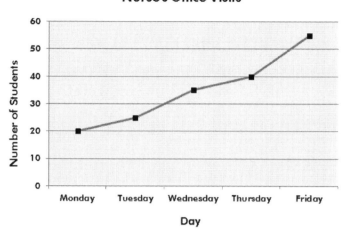

Nurse's Office Visits

Ⓐ 30 students
Ⓑ 35 students
Ⓒ 40 students
Ⓓ 45 students

8. The fourth grade chorus is selling candy boxes to raise money for a trip to the water park. The pictograph below shows how many candy boxes they sold during the first four weeks of the sale. Use the information shown in the graph to respond to the following.
The chorus needed to sell 150 boxes of candy to pay for the trip. Did they sell enough boxes?

Candy Boxes Sold

Week 1	☐ ☐ ☐ ☐
Week 2	☐ ☐ ☐ ◿
Week 3	☐ ☐ ◿
Week 4	☐ ☐ ☐ ☐ ☐ ◿

Key : ☐ = 10 boxes
◿ = 5 boxes

Ⓐ Yes, they sold more than enough boxes.
Ⓑ Yes, they sold exactly 150 boxes.
Ⓒ No, they needed to sell 5 more boxes.
Ⓓ No, they needed to sell 10 more boxes.

9. The fourth grade chorus is selling candy boxes to raise money for a trip to the water park. The pictograph below shows how many candy boxes they sold during the first four weeks of the sale. Use the information shown in the graph to respond to the following.
   How many more candy boxes were sold during the fourth week than during the first week?

Candy Boxes Sold

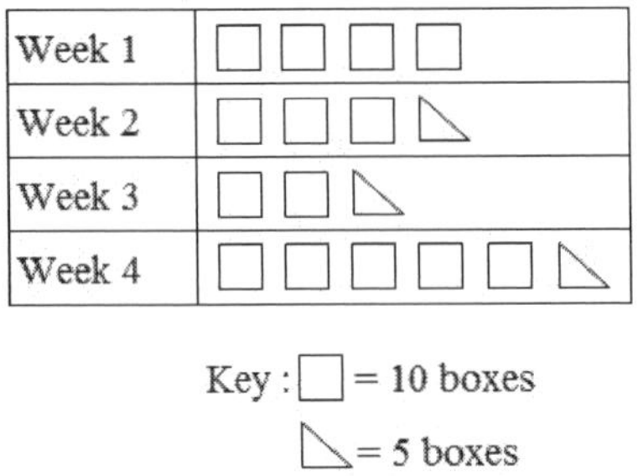

Week 1	□ □ □ □
Week 2	□ □ □ ◹
Week 3	□ □ ◹
Week 4	□ □ □ □ □ ◹

Key : □ = 10 boxes
       ◹ = 5 boxes

A 25 boxes
B 15 boxes
C 5 boxes
D None of the above

10. The fourth grade chorus is selling candy boxes to raise money for a trip to the water park. The pictograph below shows how many candy boxes they sold during the first four weeks of the sale. Use the information shown in the graph to respond to the following.
    How many candy boxes were sold during the first two weeks of the sale?

Candy Boxes Sold

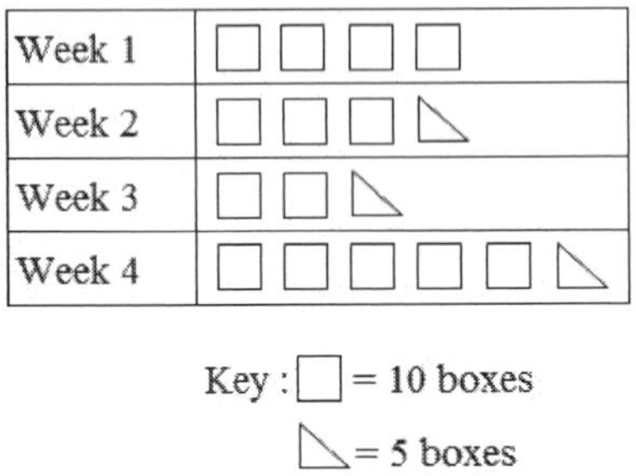

Week 1	□ □ □ □
Week 2	□ □ □ ◹
Week 3	□ □ ◹
Week 4	□ □ □ □ □ ◹

Key : □ = 10 boxes
       ◹ = 5 boxes

A $7\frac{1}{2}$ boxes
B 40 boxes
C 35 boxes
D 75 boxes

11. Mr. Green's class spent 5 weeks collecting cans as part of a recycling project. The bar graph shows how many cans they collected each week. Use the graph to respond to the following question.
How many cans were collected during the second week?

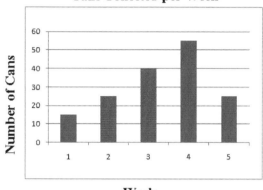

Ⓐ 15 cans
Ⓑ 20 cans
Ⓒ 25 cans
Ⓓ 35 cans

12. Mr. Green's class spent 5 weeks collecting cans as part of a recycling project. The bar graph shows how many cans they collected each week. Use the graph to respond to the following question.
How many more cans were collected during the third week than during the second week?

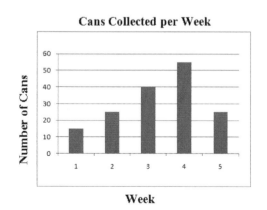

Ⓐ 5 cans
Ⓑ 15 cans
Ⓒ 25 cans
Ⓓ 40 cans

13. Mr. Green's class spent 5 weeks collecting cans as part of a recycling project. The bar graph shows how many cans they collected each week. Use the graph to respond to the following question.
    How many cans were collected during the fourth week?

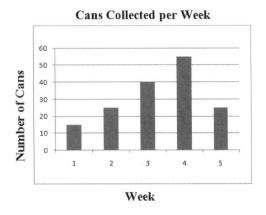

Ⓐ 65 cans
Ⓑ 55 cans
Ⓒ 50 cans
Ⓓ 40 cans

14. Mr. Green's class spent 5 weeks collecting cans as part of a recycling project. The bar graph shows how many cans they collected each week. Use the graph to respond to the following question.
    During which week were the fewest cans collected?

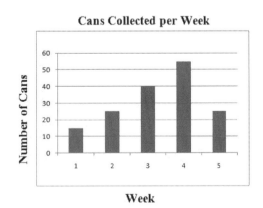

Ⓐ Week 1
Ⓑ Week 2
Ⓒ Week 3
Ⓓ Week 4

15. Mr. Green's class spent 5 weeks collecting cans as part of a recycling project. The bar graph shows how many cans they collected each week. Use the graph to respond to the following question.

During which two weeks were the same number of cans collected?

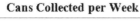

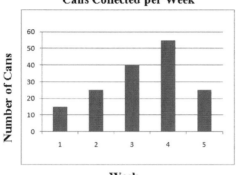

Ⓐ Weeks 1 and 2
Ⓑ Weeks 2 and 4
Ⓒ Weeks 3 and 5
Ⓓ Weeks 2 and 5

16. The students in the third grade were surveyed to find out their favorite seasons. The results are shown in the tally table. Use the tally table to respond to the following.

Which season was chosen as the favorite of the most students?

Our Favorite Seasons

Winter	╫╫ ╫╫ ╫╫ ll
Spring	╫╫ ll
Summer	╫╫ ╫╫ ╫╫ lll
Fall	lll

Ⓐ Winter
Ⓑ Spring
Ⓒ Summer
Ⓓ Fall

17. The students in the third grade were surveyed to find out their favorite seasons. The results are shown in the tally table. Use the tally table to respond to the following.
How many students chose winter as their favorite season?

Our Favorite Seasons

Winter	‖‖‖ ‖‖‖ ‖‖‖ ‖
Spring	‖‖‖ ‖
Summer	‖‖‖ ‖‖‖ ‖‖‖ ‖‖‖
Fall	‖‖‖

Ⓐ 12 students
Ⓑ 16 students
Ⓒ 17 students
Ⓓ 22 students

18. The students in the third grade were surveyed to find out their favorite seasons. The results are shown in the tally table. Use the tally table to respond to the following.
How many more students chose winter than spring?

Our Favorite Seasons

Winter	‖‖‖ ‖‖‖ ‖‖‖ ‖
Spring	‖‖‖ ‖
Summer	‖‖‖ ‖‖‖ ‖‖‖ ‖‖‖
Fall	‖‖‖

Ⓐ 5 students
Ⓑ 10 students
Ⓒ 15 students
Ⓓ 17 students

19 The students in the third grade were surveyed to find out their favorite seasons. The re-sults are shown in the tally table. Use the tally table to respond to the following.
How many students were surveyed?

Our Favorite Seasons

Winter	ＴＨＬ ＴＨＬ ＴＨＬ ＩＩ
Spring	ＴＨＬ ＩＩ
Summer	ＴＨＬ ＴＨＬ ＴＨＬ ＩＩＩ
Fall	ＩＩＩ

Ⓐ 40 students
Ⓑ 45 students
Ⓒ 50 students
Ⓓ 55 students

20. Teachers at a nearby elementary school took a survey to determine how to plan for fu-ture field trips. What is the sum of the field trip choices that received the highest votes?

Field Trips	No. of Votes
Jersey Cape	11
turtle Back Zoo	7
camden's Children Garden	8
NJ Adventure Aquarium	11

Ⓐ 19
Ⓑ 18
Ⓒ 22
Ⓓ 15

21. The chart shows the range of snowfall expected each month at a local ski resort. During which month is there the greatest range in the amount of snowfall?

Month	Inches of Snow Fall
November	0 - 5
December	5 - 15
January	10 - 50
February	10 - 20

Ⓐ November
Ⓑ December
Ⓒ January
Ⓓ February

22. Based on the bar graph below, what can be said about the trend in bicycle helmet safety?

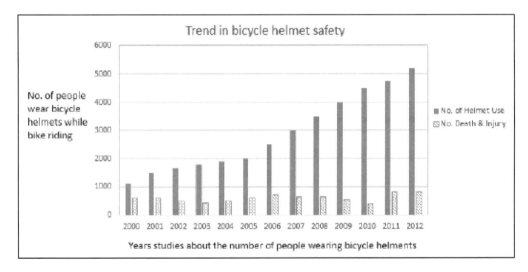

Ⓐ Bicycle riders who do not wear helmets are very unlikely to be injured or killed.
Ⓑ Bicycle riders who wear helmets are very unlikely to be injured or killed.
Ⓒ Wearing a helmet has no effect on bicycle safety.
Ⓓ Wearing a helmet affects bicycle safety on occasions.

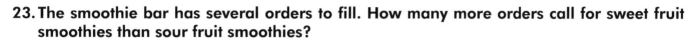
23. The smoothie bar has several orders to fill. How many more orders call for sweet fruit smoothies than sour fruit smoothies?

Orders Call	Sweet Fruit Smoothies	Sour Fruit Smoothies
Ron Miller	10	2
Robert	5	5
George	4	3
Mike	6	4
Marisa	3	2
Greg	1	2

- Ⓐ 23
- Ⓑ 11
- Ⓒ 12
- Ⓓ 35

24. The line plot below shows the lengths of fish caught.

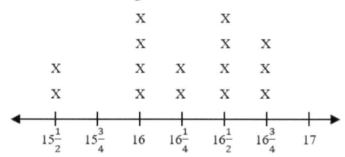

Lengths of Fish

Instruction: The line plot shows the data rounded to the nearest $\frac{1}{4}$ inch.

How much longer is the longest fish than the shortest fish? Drag and drop your answer into the box.

- Ⓐ $1\frac{1}{2}$
- Ⓑ $2\frac{1}{4}$
- Ⓒ $1\frac{1}{4}$
- Ⓓ $1\frac{3}{4}$

25. The line plot given below shows the lengths of fish caught. Find the total length if all the fish measuring $16\frac{1}{2}$ inches in length were to be laid end to end? Drag your answer into the box.

Lengths of Fish

```
                    X           X
                    X           X    X
        X           X    X      X    X
        X           X    X      X    X
  ◄─────┼────┼─────┼────┼─────┼────┼─────┼─────►
      15 1/2  15 3/4  16   16 1/4  16 1/2  16 3/4  17
```

Ⓐ 68 inches
Ⓑ 66 inches
Ⓒ 62 inches
Ⓓ 64 inches

26. Match each statement with the type of graph used for interpreting the data in each situation.

	Bar graph	Line graph	Pie Chart
The results of the number of boys in each grade.	◯	◯	◯
The percentage of favorite desserts of the students in the class	◯	◯	◯
The price of a car over the years.	◯	◯	◯

27. Which group has the largest number of people in it? Write your answer in the box below

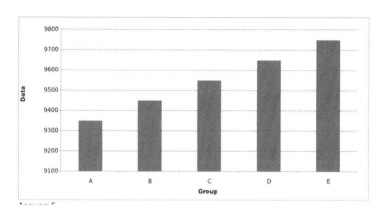

28. The line plot below shows the amount of sugar in 6 popular candy bars.

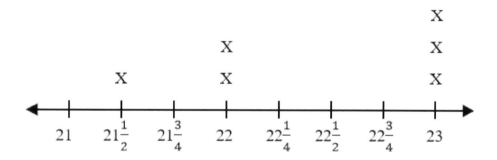

Instruction: The line plot shows the data rounded to the nearest $\frac{1}{2}$ g.
How many total grams of sugar are in all 6 candy bars combined? Circle the correct answer.

Ⓐ $55\frac{1}{2}$ grams

Ⓑ $80\frac{1}{2}$ grams

Ⓒ $113\frac{1}{2}$ grams

Ⓓ $134\frac{1}{2}$ grams

29. Plot the number of people liking caramel apples, corn dogs and french fries in the form of a bar graph.

Favorite Carnival Foods

caramel apples	elephant ears	corn dogs	cotton candy	french fries	candy apples	funnel cakes
X			X			
X			X		X	X
X			X		X	X
X			X		X	X
X		X	X		X	X
X		X	X		X	X
X	X	X	X		X	X
X	X	X	X		X	X
X	X	X	X	X	X	X
X	X	X	X	X	X	X
X	X	X	X	X	X	X

30. Match the number of people liking the food to the correct category.

Each x represents 1 person

Favorite Carnival Foods

caramel apples	elephant ears	corn dogs	cotton candy	french fries	candy apples	funnel cakes
x			x			
x			x		x	x
x			x		x	x
x			x		x	x
x		x	x		x	x
x		x	x		x	x
x	x	x	x		x	x
x	x	x	x		x	x
x	x	x	x	x	x	x
x	x	x	x	x	x	x
x	x	x	x	x	x	x

Candy Apples --------------- ( )

Elephant Years --------------- ( )

Cotton Candy---------------- ( )

Corn Candy ----------------- ( )

Chapter 5

Lesson 5: Angle Measurement

You can scan the QR code given below or use the url to access additional EdSearch resources including videos and mobile apps related to *Angle Measurement*.

ed Search   *Angle Measurement*

URL	QR Code
http://www.lumoslearning.com/a/4mdc5a	

1. In the figure below, two lines intersect to form ∠A, ∠B, ∠C, and ∠D.
    If ∠C measures 128°, then ∠A measures:

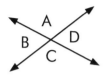

Ⓐ 52°
Ⓑ 128°
Ⓒ 90°
Ⓓ 180°

2. In the figure below, two lines intersect to form ∠A, ∠B, ∠C, and ∠D.
    If ∠C measures 128°, then ∠D measures:

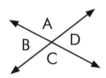

Ⓐ 52°
Ⓑ 128°
Ⓒ 90°
Ⓓ 180°

3. In the figure below, two lines intersect to form ∠A, ∠B, ∠C, and ∠D.
    If ∠B measures 68°, then ∠D measures:

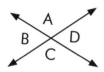

Ⓐ 152°
Ⓑ 90°
Ⓒ 180°
Ⓓ 68°

4. If the measurement of ∠A is 64°, then what is the measurement of ∠B?

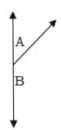

Ⓐ 126°
Ⓑ 119°
Ⓒ 116°
Ⓓ 64°

5. If the measurement of ∠B is 94°, then what is the measurement of ∠A?

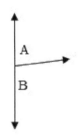

Ⓐ 90°
Ⓑ 86°
Ⓒ 66°
Ⓓ 94°

6 The total of the measures of ∠A and ∠B equals 90°. If ∠A measures 51°, then what does ∠B measure?

Ⓐ 139°
Ⓑ 51°
Ⓒ 49°
Ⓓ 39°

7. Two supplementary angles should total _____.

   Ⓐ 90°
   Ⓑ 45°
   Ⓒ 180°
   Ⓓ 360°

8. What should two complementary angles add up to?

   Ⓐ 45°
   Ⓑ 90°
   Ⓒ 180°
   Ⓓ 360°

9. Complete the sentence:
   The measure of an obtuse angle is _____.

   Ⓐ less than the measure of a right angle
   Ⓑ equal to the measure of a right angle
   Ⓒ greater than the measure of a right angle
   Ⓓ less than the measure of an acute angle

10. What is the measure of the complement of an angle that measures 7°?

    Ⓐ 173°
    Ⓑ 87°
    Ⓒ 83°
    Ⓓ 73°

11. What is the measure of ∠A if ∠B measures 46° ?

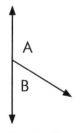

    Ⓐ 134°
    Ⓑ 143°
    Ⓒ 44°
    Ⓓ 90°

12. If ∠A measures 101° and ∠B measures 49° then what does ∠C measure?

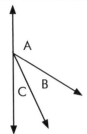

Ⓐ 150°
Ⓑ 20°
Ⓒ 40°
Ⓓ 30°

13. What is the supplement of an angle that measures 73°?

Ⓐ 117°
Ⓑ 107°
Ⓒ 23°
Ⓓ 17°

14. What is the measurement of each of the angles in this equilateral triangle?

Ⓐ 45°
Ⓑ 60°
Ⓒ 90°
Ⓓ 180°

15. If ∠A measures 45° and ∠C measures 45° then what does ∠B measure?

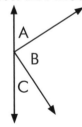

Ⓐ 45°
Ⓑ 75°
Ⓒ 90°
Ⓓ 135°

16. What is the angle measurement for the angle shown below? Write your answer in the box given below.

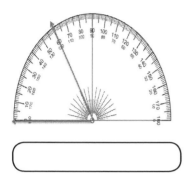

```
(                    )
```

17. What is the angle measurement for the below angle? Type the number in the box.

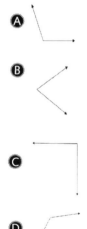

RIGHT ANGLE

```
(                    )
```
degree

18. Which angles are obtuse angles? Select all the correct answers.

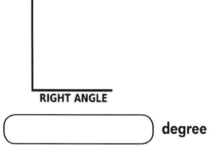

Ⓐ

Ⓑ

Ⓒ

Ⓓ

19. 1° is defined as 1/360 of a whole turn. What fraction of a whole turn is 45°?

Ⓐ 1/4
Ⓑ 1/8
Ⓒ 1/12
Ⓓ 1/6

Chapter 5

Lesson 6: Measuring Turned Angles

You can scan the QR code given below or use the url to access additional EdSearch resources including videos and mobile apps related to *Measuring Turned Angles*.

ed Search	*Measuring Turned Angles*	
URL		**QR Code**
http://www.lumoslearning.com/a/4mdc5b		

1. **At ice skating lessons, Erika attempts to do a 360 degree spin, but she only manages a half turn on her first attempt. How many degrees short of her goal was Erika's first attempt?**

   Ⓐ 90 degrees
   Ⓑ 180 degrees
   Ⓒ 0 degrees
   Ⓓ 360 degrees

2. **Erika's sister, Melanie, attempts to do a 360 degree turn, just like her sister, but she made a quarter turn on her first attempt. How many degrees short of her goal was Melanie's first attempt?**

   Ⓐ 180 degrees
   Ⓑ 90 degrees
   Ⓒ 270 degrees
   Ⓓ 280 degrees

3. **A water sprinkler covers 90 degrees of the Brown's backyard lawn. How many times will the sprinkler need to be moved in order to cover the full 360 degrees of the lawn?**

   Ⓐ 4
   Ⓑ 2
   Ⓒ 3
   Ⓓ 5

4. **A ceiling fan rotates 80 degrees and then it stops. How many more degrees does it need to rotate in order to make a full rotation?**

   Ⓐ 265 degrees
   Ⓑ 90 degrees
   Ⓒ 180 degrees
   Ⓓ 280 degrees

5. **Trixie is a professional photographer. She uses software on her computer to edit some wedding photos. She rotates the photograph of the bride 120 clockwise. Then she rotates it another 140 degrees clockwise. If she continues rotating the photo clockwise, how many more degrees will Trixie need to turn it to have made a complete 360 degree turn?**

   Ⓐ 100 degrees
   Ⓑ 90 degrees
   Ⓒ 180 degrees
   Ⓓ 120 degrees

6. What is the angle measurement for the below angle? Type the number in the box.

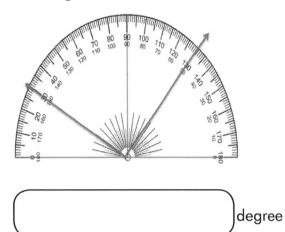

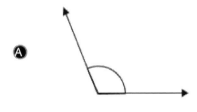 degree

7. Which angles are reflex angles? Select all the correct answers.

Ⓐ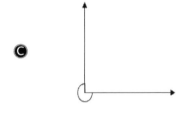

Ⓑ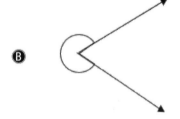

Ⓒ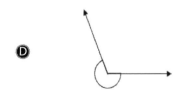

Ⓓ

8. When the measures of two angles A and B are added, you get 430 degrees. If the measure of angle A is 120 degrees, what is the measure of angle B? Circle the correct answer.

Ⓐ 320°
Ⓑ 310°
Ⓒ 210°
Ⓓ 550°

Chapter 5

Lesson 7: Measuring and Sketching Angles

You can scan the QR code given below or use the url to access additional EdSearch resources including videos and mobile apps related to *Measuring and Sketching Angles*.

 **Measuring and Sketching Angles**

URL	QR Code
http://www.lumoslearning.com/a/4mdc6	

1. What is the measure of angle JKL?

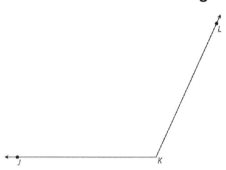

Ⓐ 65 degrees
Ⓑ 115 degrees
Ⓒ 75 degrees
Ⓓ 140 degrees

2. What is the measure of this angle?

Ⓐ 10 degrees
Ⓑ 28 degrees
Ⓒ 48 degrees
Ⓓ 90 degrees

3. What is the measure of angle PQR?

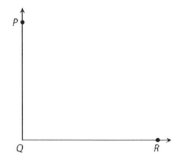

Ⓐ 360 degrees
Ⓑ 180 degrees
Ⓒ 0 degrees
Ⓓ 90 degrees

4. **What is the measure of the interior angles of this shape?**

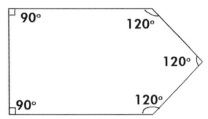

90°   120°

120°

90°   120°

Ⓐ 400 degrees
Ⓑ 360 degrees
Ⓒ 540 degrees
Ⓓ 520 degrees

5. **What can you use to help measure angles?**

Ⓐ a degree
Ⓑ a protractor
Ⓒ a vertex
Ⓓ an angle

6. **What is the angle measurement for the below angle? Write the answer in the box below.**

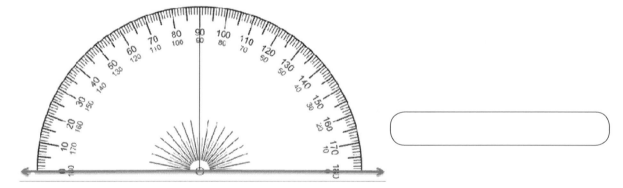

7. **What is the angle measurement for the below angle? Write the answer in the box below.**

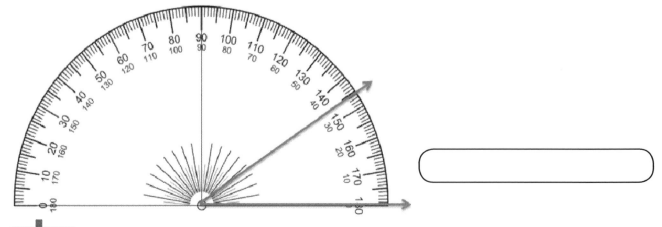

8. What fraction of a whole turn is a straight angle? Circle the correct answer.

   Ⓐ 1/2
   Ⓑ 1/4
   Ⓒ 3/4
   Ⓓ 5/8

9. Which angle is equal to 1/6 of a whole turn? Shade the figure below to represent the answer.

   Instruction : 1 shaded cell = 10 degrees.

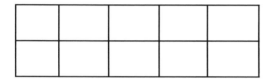

Chapter 5

Lesson 8: Adding and Subtracting Angle Measurements

You can scan the QR code given below or use the url to access additional EdSearch resources including videos and mobile apps related to *Adding and Subtracting Angle Measurements*.

ed)Search ***Adding and Subtracting Angle Measurements***

URL	QR Code
http://www.lumoslearning.com/a/4mdc7	

1. Angle 1 measures 40 degrees, and angle 2 measures 30 degrees. What is the measure of the angle of PQR?

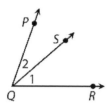

   Ⓐ 70 degrees
   Ⓑ 80 degrees
   Ⓒ 100 degrees
   Ⓓ 10 degrees

2. Angle ADC measures 120 degrees, and angle ADB measures 95 degrees. What is the measure of the angle BDC?

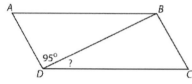

   Ⓐ 5 degrees
   Ⓑ 35 degrees
   Ⓒ 15 degrees
   Ⓓ 25 degrees

3. Angle JNM measures 100 degrees, angle JNK measures 25 degrees, and angle KNL measures 35 degrees. What is the measure of the angle LNM?

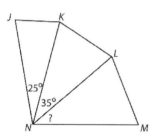

   Ⓐ 35 degrees
   Ⓑ 40 degrees
   Ⓒ 30 degrees
   Ⓓ 25 degrees

4. **What fraction of a circle is a 180 degree angle?**

   Ⓐ $\dfrac{1}{4}$

   Ⓑ $\dfrac{1}{2}$

   Ⓒ $\dfrac{1}{3}$

   Ⓓ $\dfrac{1}{5}$

5. **What fraction of a circle is a 90 degree angle?**

   Ⓐ $\dfrac{1}{4}$

   Ⓑ $\dfrac{1}{2}$

   Ⓒ $\dfrac{1}{3}$

   Ⓓ $\dfrac{1}{5}$

6. **What is the angle measurement for the below angles when subtracted? Write the answer in the box shown below**

RIGHT ANGLE

45°

7. **What is the value of x° and y° in the figure below. Circle the correct answer**

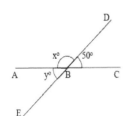

   Ⓐ x° = 120° and y° = 60°
   Ⓑ x° = 130° and y° = 50°
   Ⓒ x° = 50° and y° = 130°
   Ⓓ x° = 110° and y° = 70°

End of Measurement & Data

Chapter 6: Geometry

Lesson 1: Points, Lines, Rays, and Segments

You can scan the QR code given below or use the url to access additional EdSearch resources including videos and mobile apps related to *Points, Lines, Ray, and Segments.*

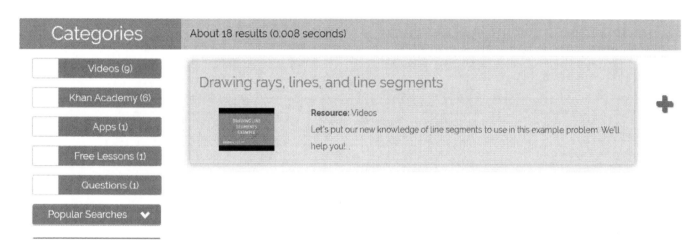

Categories   About 18 results (0.008 seconds)

Videos (9)

Khan Academy (6)   **Drawing rays, lines, and line segments**

Apps (1)   **Resource:** Videos

Free Lessons (1)   Let's put our new knowledge of line segments to use in this example problem. We'll

Questions (1)   help you!..

Popular Searches ⌄

ed Search   ***Points, Lines, Rays, and Segments***

URL	QR Code
http://www.lumoslearning.com/a/4ga1	

1. **Which of the following is a quadrilateral?**

    Ⓐ Triangle
    Ⓑ Rhombus
    Ⓒ Pentagon
    Ⓓ Hexagon

2. **How many sides does a pentagon have?**

    Ⓐ 3
    Ⓑ 2
    Ⓒ 1
    Ⓓ 5

3. **Use the network below to respond to the following question: How many line segments connect directly to Vertex F?**

    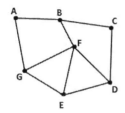

    Ⓐ 3
    Ⓑ 4
    Ⓒ 5
    Ⓓ 6

4. **Which of these statements is true?**

    Ⓐ A parallelogram must be a rectangle.
    Ⓑ A trapezoid might be a square.
    Ⓒ A rhombus must be a trapezoid.
    Ⓓ A rectangle must be a parallelogram.

5. **What is being shown below?**

    ⟷
    ⟷

    Ⓐ a pair of parallel lines
    Ⓑ a pair of intersecting lines
    Ⓒ a pair of congruent rays
    Ⓓ a pair of perpendicular lines

6. **What is being shown below?**

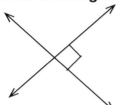

- Ⓐ a pair of parallel lines
- Ⓑ a pair of perpendicular lines
- Ⓒ a pair of obtuse angles
- Ⓓ a net for a cube

7. **Identify the following plane figures.**

- Ⓐ heptagon and quadrilateral
- Ⓑ hexagon and quadrilateral
- Ⓒ octagon and quadrilateral
- Ⓓ octagon and pentagon

8. **How many sides does an octagon have?**

- Ⓐ 8
- Ⓑ 7
- Ⓒ 6
- Ⓓ 5

9. **What kind of lines intersect to make 90 degree angles?**

- Ⓐ supplementary
- Ⓑ perpendicular
- Ⓒ skew
- Ⓓ parallel

10. **How many right angles does a parallelogram have?**

- Ⓐ 0
- Ⓑ 2
- Ⓒ 4
- Ⓓ It depends on the type of parallelogram.

11. Circle the 'Point' from the figures.

Ⓐ

Ⓑ

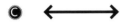

Ⓒ

Ⓓ   •

12. How many end points does a segment have? Write your answer in the box below.

13. With reference to the figure below, which of the following statements are correct? Select all the correct answers.

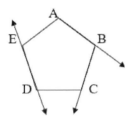

Ⓐ There are 2 rays.
Ⓑ There are 3 line segments.
Ⓒ There is one line.
Ⓓ There is no line.

Name _____   Date _____

Chapter 6

Lesson 2: Angles

You can scan the QR code given below or use the url to access additional EdSearch resources including videos and mobile apps related to *Angles*.

 **Angles**

URL	QR Code
http://www.lumoslearning.com/a/4ga1	

1. The hands of this clock form a(n) _____ angle.

   Ⓐ obtuse
   Ⓑ straight
   Ⓒ right
   Ⓓ acute

2. How many acute angles and obtuse angles are there in the figure shown below?

   Ⓐ 2 acute angles and 6 obtuse angles
   Ⓑ 4 acute angles and 4 obtuse angles
   Ⓒ 8 acute angles and 0 obtuse angles
   Ⓓ 0 acute angles and 8 obtuse angles

3. Describe the angles found in this figure.

   Ⓐ 2 right angles and 3 acute angles
   Ⓑ 3 right angles and 2 obtuse angles
   Ⓒ 2 right angles, 2 obtuse angles, and 1 acute angle
   Ⓓ 2 right angles and 3 obtuse angles

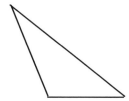
4. What type of triangle is shown below?

Ⓐ Isosceles triangle
Ⓑ Scalene triangle
Ⓒ Equilateral triangle
Ⓓ None of the above

5. Which statement is true about an obtuse angle?

Ⓐ It measures less than 90 degrees.
Ⓑ It measures more than 90 degrees.
Ⓒ It measures exactly 90 degrees.
Ⓓ It measures more than 180 degrees.

6. Which statement is true about a straight angle?

Ⓐ It measures less than 90 degrees.
Ⓑ It measures more than 90 degrees.
Ⓒ It measures exactly 90 degrees.
Ⓓ It measures exactly 180 degrees.

7. A square has what type of angles?

Ⓐ 2 acute and 2 right angles
Ⓑ 4 right angles
Ⓒ 4 acute angles
Ⓓ It depends on the size of the square.

8. Which statement is true about an equilateral triangle.

Ⓐ It has 1 acute angle and 2 obtuse angles.
Ⓑ It has 2 acute angles and 1 right angle.
Ⓒ It has all 30 degree angles.
Ⓓ It has all 60 degree angles.

9. **Classify the angle:**

Ⓐ right
Ⓑ acute
Ⓒ obtuse
Ⓓ straight

10. Tina wanted her bedroom area rug to be designed after a geometric shape. The rug has somewhat of a circular shape with 7 straight sides and 7 obtuse angles. What is the name of this shape?

Ⓐ hexagon
Ⓑ octagon
Ⓒ pentagon
Ⓓ heptagon

11. **Select all the obtuse angles.**

 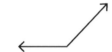

12. **How many of the following angles are right angles? Write your answer in the box below.**

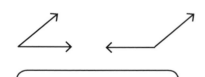

13. **Choose the letters among the following which have at least one right angle. Note that there may be more than one correct answer.**

Ⓐ L
Ⓑ T
Ⓒ V
Ⓓ E

Chapter 6

Lesson 3: Classifying Plane (2-D) Shapes

You can scan the QR code given below or use the url to access additional EdSearch resources including videos and mobile apps related to *Classifying Plane (2-D) Shapes*.

 **Search**   *Classifying Plane (2-D) Shapes*

URL	QR Code
http://www.lumoslearning.com/a/4ga2	

1. **Complete the sentence:**
   A polygon is named based on _____ .

   Ⓐ how many sides or interior angles it has
   Ⓑ how many of its sides are straight
   Ⓒ how large it is
   Ⓓ how many lines of symmetry it has

2. **Complete the sentence:**
   A polygon with 4 sides and 4 interior angles is called a(n) _____ .

   Ⓐ triangle
   Ⓑ quadrilateral
   Ⓒ pentagon
   Ⓓ octagon

3. **Complete the sentence:**
   A rectangle must have _____ .

   Ⓐ all parallel sides and all congruent sides
   Ⓑ 2 pairs of parallel sides and 2 pairs of congruent sides
   Ⓒ 2 pairs of parallel sides and 4 congruent sides
   Ⓓ 4 parallel sides and 2 pairs of congruent sides

4. **Complete the sentence:**
   A polygon must have _____ .

   Ⓐ 3 or more interior angles
   Ⓑ at least one pair of parallel sides
   Ⓒ at least one pair of congruent sides
   Ⓓ a line of symmetry

5. **Classify this triangle:**

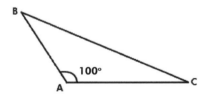

   Ⓐ acute triangle
   Ⓑ obtuse triangle
   Ⓒ right triangle
   Ⓓ straight triangle

6. **If the angles on a triangle all measure less than 90 degrees, what type of triangle is it?**

  Ⓐ obtuse triangle
  Ⓑ right triangle
  Ⓒ straight triangle
  Ⓓ acute triangle

7. **Another name form a 180 degree angle is a(n) _____.**

  Ⓐ right angle
  Ⓑ obtuse angle
  Ⓒ straight angle
  Ⓓ acute angle

8. **Complete the sentence:**
   A point has _____.

  Ⓐ size but no position
  Ⓑ size and position
  Ⓒ neither size nor position
  Ⓓ position but no size

9. **Name the angle found at the corners of the swimming pool shown below.**

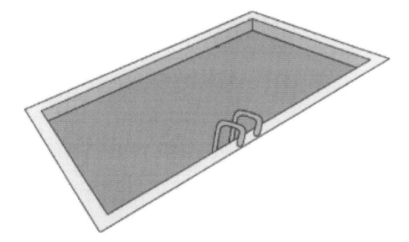

  Ⓐ Angles found at the corners of the swimming pool consist of acute angles.
  Ⓑ Angles found at the corners of the swimming pool consist of straight angles.
  Ⓒ Angles found at the corners of the swimming pool consist of right angles.
  Ⓓ Angles found at the corners of the swimming pool consist of obtuse angles.

10. Classify the triangles shown in this design.

Ⓐ They are acute triangles.
Ⓑ They are right triangles.
Ⓒ They are obtuse triangles.
Ⓓ They are straight triangles.

11. Select all the pentagons by circling them.

12. How many triangles are listed below? Write your answer in the box below.

Name _____   Date _____

13. In the first column, classification of the triangles based on the lengths of the sides is given. Select all possible triangles for each type of triangle. (if the answer is "possible" select that option by ticking the option)

	can be an acute triangle	can be an obtuse triangle	can be a right triangle
An equilateral triangle	☐	☐	☐
An isosceles triangle	☐	☐	☐
A scalene triangle	☐	☐	☐

14. For each statement given in the first column, select true, if it is correct or select false, if it is wrong.

	True	False
An acute triangle can be an equilateral triangle	○	○
An acute triangle cannot be an isosceles triangle	○	○
An acute triangle cannot be a scalene triangle	○	○
All right triangles are scalene triangles	○	○
An obtuse triangle can be an isosceles triangle	○	○
An obtuse triangle can be a scalene triangle	○	○

Chapter 6

Lesson 4: Symmetry

You can scan the QR code given below or use the url to access additional EdSearch resources including videos and mobile apps related to *Symmetry*.

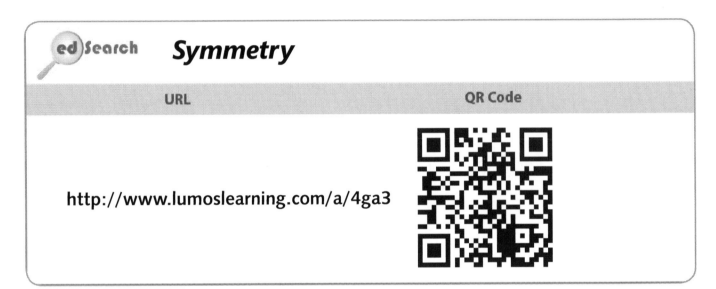

URL	QR Code
http://www.lumoslearning.com/a/4ga3	

1. How many lines of symmetry does an equilateral triangle have?

   Ⓐ 1
   Ⓑ 3
   Ⓒ 2
   Ⓓ 0

2. How many lines of symmetry does a regular pentagon have?

   Ⓐ 1
   Ⓑ 2
   Ⓒ 5
   Ⓓ 10

3. How many lines of symmetry does a rectangle have?

   Ⓐ 1
   Ⓑ 2
   Ⓒ 3
   Ⓓ 4

4. How many lines of symmetry does a regular octagon have?

   Ⓐ 2
   Ⓑ 4
   Ⓒ 6
   Ⓓ 8

5. How many lines of symmetry does a square have?

   Ⓐ 2
   Ⓑ 4
   Ⓒ 6
   Ⓓ 8

6. How many lines of symmetry does a parallelogram have if it is not a square, rectangle, or rhombus?

   Ⓐ 2
   Ⓑ 4
   Ⓒ 1
   Ⓓ 0

7. **How many lines of symmetry does the following object have?**

Ⓐ 0
Ⓑ 2
Ⓒ 4
Ⓓ 6

8. **How many lines of symmetry does the following object have?**

Ⓐ 0
Ⓑ 1
Ⓒ 2
Ⓓ 3

9. **How many lines of symmetry does the following shape have?**

Ⓐ 4
Ⓑ 3
Ⓒ 2
Ⓓ 1

10. Regular rectangles have 4 angles and 4 lines of symmetry. Regular pentagons have 5 angles and 5 lines of symmetry. Regular hexagons have 6 angles and 6 lines of symmetry. If this pattern were to continue, how many lines of symmetry does a regular heptagon have?

Ⓐ 7
Ⓑ 8
Ⓒ 3
Ⓓ 2

11. Select the heart with the correct line of symmetry below by circling it.

12. Select the figures with the correct lines of symmetry. Note that more than one option may be correct. Select all the correct answers.

 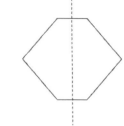

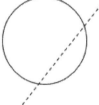

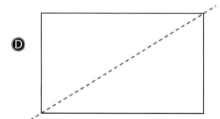

End of Geometry

MAAP FAQs

What will MAAP Assessment Look Like?

In many ways, the MAAP assessments will be unlike anything many students have ever seen. The tests will be conducted online, requiring students complete tasks to assess a deeper understanding of the College-and Career Ready Standards (MCCRS). The students will take the Grade level Assessment at the end of the year.

For MAAP Math Test, the details are as below:

Grade Band	Session 1		Session 2
	Questions	Time (in Minutes)	Time (in Minutes)
3-5	46	127	70
6-8	58	157	90

How is this Lumos tedBook aligned to MAAP Guidelines?

The practice tests provided in the Lumos Program were created to reflect the depth and rigor of the MAAP assessments based on the information published by the test administrator. However, the content and format of the MAAP assessment that is officially administered to the students could be different compared to these practice tests. You can get more information about this test by visiting http://www.mde.k12.ms.us/OSA/MAAP

What item types are included in the Online MAAP Test?

Mississippi Academic Assessment Program(MAAP) Test include:

- Open ended items
- Close ended items
- Performance tests

For more information on 2021-22 Assessment year, visit
http://www.lumoslearning.com/a/maap-2021-faqs
OR Scan the **QR Code**

For MAAP ELA Tests:

Close-ended items include
- Multi-choice static (MC)
- Multi-choice dynamic (MCD) - Uses drag and drop into boxes
- Multi choice multi select (MCMS)

Open-ended items include
- Multi select table (MST),
- Select Text (ST),
- Drag & drop (DD),
- Matching (M),
- Two part (2P)
- Type in text

Performance Task:
The Performance Task for English Language Arts is a written response to a writing prompt. The Students will read a text and respond to a prompt using evidence from the text. The extended responses will be human scored using a rubric.

The rubric is comprised of three categories: Development of Ideas, Organization, and Language, Usage, and Conventions. The Performance Tasks are worth 12 points total.

For MAAP Math Tests

Close-ended items include
- Multi-choice static (MC)
- Multi-choice dynamic (MCD) - Uses drag and drop into boxes
- Multi choice multi select (MCMS)
- Graphing- Line graphs (GL)
- Graphing – Bar Graphs (GB)

Open-ended items include
- Multi select table (MST),
- Select Text (ST),
- Drag & drop (DD),
- Two part (2P)
- Matching (M)
- Type in text

Performance Task:
The Mathematics, Grades 3-8 End of Course performance task tests students knowledge, precision, interpretation skills, conceptual understanding which can be measured and related to creating, analyzing and using functions to real world phenomena. The Performance task will include graphic display and series of written arguments that will measure the student's proficiency level from the Mathematics, Grades 3-8 content standards.

The Grade-Level Assessments include multiple types of questions or items:

1. Drag and Drop
2. Evidence Based Selected Response (EBSR)
3. Extended Constructed Response
4. Hot Text Selective Highlight
5. Multiple Choice, Single Answer
6. Multiple Choice, Multiple Answer
7. Numeric Response
8. Drop Down Equation
9. Matching Table

Discover Engaging and Relevant Learning Resources

Lumos EdSearch is a safe search engine specifically designed for teachers and students. Using EdSearch, you can easily find thousands of standards-aligned learning resources such as questions, videos, lessons, worksheets and apps. Teachers can use EdSearch to create custom resource kits to perfectly match their lesson objective and assign them to one or more students in their classroom.

To access the EdSearch tool, use the search box after you log into Lumos StepUp or use the link provided below.

http://www.lumoslearning.com/a/edsearchb	

The Lumos Standards Coherence map provides information about previous level, next level and related standards. It helps educators and students visually explore learning standards. It's an effective tool to help students progress through the learning objectives. Teachers can use this tool to develop their own pacing charts and lesson plans. Educators can also use the coherence map to get deep insights into why a student is struggling in a specific learning objective.

Teachers can access the Coherence maps after logging into the StepUp Teacher Portal or use the link provided below.

http://www.lumoslearning.com/a/coherence-map	

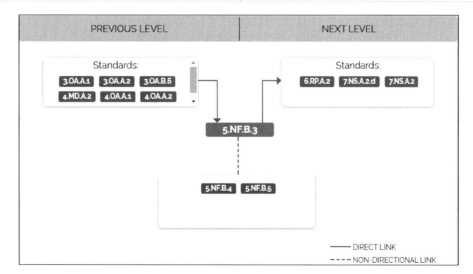

What if I buy more than one Lumos Study Program?

Step 1

Visit the URL and login to your account.
http://www.lumoslearning.com

Step 2

Click on 'My tedBooks' under the "Account" tab.
Place the Book Access Code and submit.

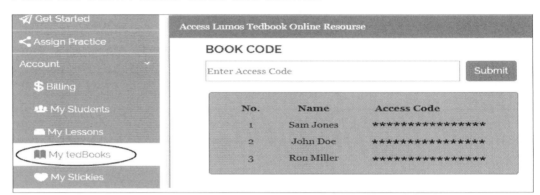

Step 3

To add the new book for a registered student, choose the
⦿ Existing Student button and select the student and submit.

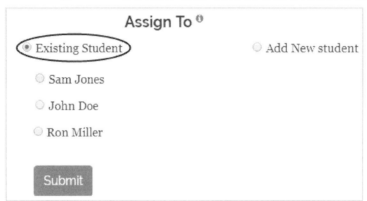

To add the new book for a new student, choose the ⦿ Add New student
button and complete the student registration.

Assign To ⓞ

○ Existing Student   ⦿ Add New student

Register Your TedBook

Student Name:*	Enter First Name	Enter Last Name
Student Login*		
Password*		

Submit

Lumos StepUp® Mobile App
FAQ For Students

What is the Lumos StepUp® App?

It is a FREE application you can download onto your Android Smartphones, tablets, iPhones, and iPads.

What are the Benefits of the StepUp® App?

This mobile application gives convenient access to Practice Tests, Common Core State Standards, Online Workbooks, and learning resources through your Smartphone and tablet computers.
- Eleven Technology enhanced question types in both MATH and ELA
- Sample questions for Arithmetic drills
- Standard specific sample questions
- Instant access to the Common Core State Standards
- Jokes and cartoons to make learning fun!

Do I Need the StepUp® App to Access Online Workbooks?

No, you can access Lumos StepUp® Online Workbooks through a personal computer. The StepUp® app simply enhances your learning experience and allows you to conveniently access StepUp® Online Workbooks and additional resources through your smartphone or tablet.

How can I Download the App?

Visit **lumoslearning.com/a/stepup-app** using your Smartphone or tablet and follow the instructions to download the app.

QR Code
for Smartphone
Or Tablet Users

Lumos StepUp® Mobile App FAQ For Parents and Teachers

What is the Lumos StepUp® App?

It is a free app that teachers can use to easily access real-time student activity information as well as assign learning resources to students. Parents can also use it to easily access school-related information such as homework assigned by teachers and PTA meetings. It can be downloaded onto smartphones and tablets from popular App Stores.

What are the Benefits of the Lumos StepUp® App?

It provides convenient access to

- Standards aligned learning resources for your students
- An easy to use Dashboard
- Student progress reports
- Active and inactive students in your classroom
- Professional development information
- Educational Blogs

How can I Download the App?

Visit **lumoslearning.com/a/stepup-app** using your Smartphone or tablet and follow the instructions to download the app.

QR Code
for Smartphone
Or Tablet Users

Progress Chart

Standard	Lesson	Page No.	Practice		Mastered	Re-practice /Reteach
MAAP			Date	Score		
4.OA.A.1	Number Sentences	10				
4.OA.A.2	Real World Problems	14				
4.OA.A.3	Multi-step Problems	18				
4.OA.B.4	Number Theory	22				
4.OA.B.5	Patterns	27				
4.NBT.A.1	Place Value	32				
4.NBT.A.2	Compare Numbers and Expanded Notation	36				
4.NBT.A.3	Rounding Numbers	40				
4.NBT.B.4	Addition & Subtraction	44				
4.NBT.B.5	Multiplication	48				
4.NBT.B.5	Division	52				
4.NF.A.1	Equivalent Fractions	56				
4.NF.A.2	Compare Fractions	62				
4.NF.B.3.A	Adding & Subtracting Fractions	68				
4.NF.B.3.B	Adding and Subtracting Fractions Through Decompositions	72				
4.NF.B.3.C	Adding and Subtracting Mixed Numbers	75				
4.NF.B.3.D	Adding and Subtracting Fractions in Word Problems	78				
4.NF.B.4.A	Multiplying Fractions	82				
4.NF.B.4.B	Multiplying Fractions by a Whole Number	85				
4.NF.B.4.C	Multiplying Fractions in Word Problems	88				
4.NF.C.5	10 to 100 Equivalent Fractions	91				
4.NF.C.6	Convert Fractions to Decimals	95				
4.NF.C.7	Compare Decimals	99				

Standard	Lesson	Page No.	Practice		Mastered	Re-practice/ Reteach
CCSS			Date	Score		
4.MD.A.1	Units of Measurement	104				
4.MD.A.2	Measurement Problems	108				
4.MD.A.3	Perimeter & Area	113				
4.MD.B.4	Representing and Interpreting Data	119				
4.MD.C.5.A	Angle Measurement	136				
4.MD.C.5.B	Measuring Turned Angles	142				
4.MD.C.6	Measuring and Sketching Angles	146				
4.MD.C.7	Adding and Subtracting Angle Measurements	150				
4.G.A.1	Points, Lines, Rays and Segments	153				
4.G.A.1	Angles	157				
4.G.A.2	Classifying Plane (2-D) Shapes	161				
4.G.A.3	Symmetry	166				

Mississippi Academic Assessment Program (MAAP) Online Assessments and Grade 4 English Language Arts Literacy (ELA) Practice Workbook, Student Copy

Lumos Learning
Developed by Expert Teachers

4 Grade

MAAP
ENGLISH
LANGUAGE ARTS LITERACY
Student Copy

Updated for 2021-22

2 MAAP Practice Tests
9 Questions Types

tedBook
ONLINE

Mississippi Department of Education does not sponsor or endorse this product.

Available
- At Leading book stores
- Online www.LumosLearning.com